AN ILLUSTRATED HISTORY OF LONDON BUSES

Kevin Lane

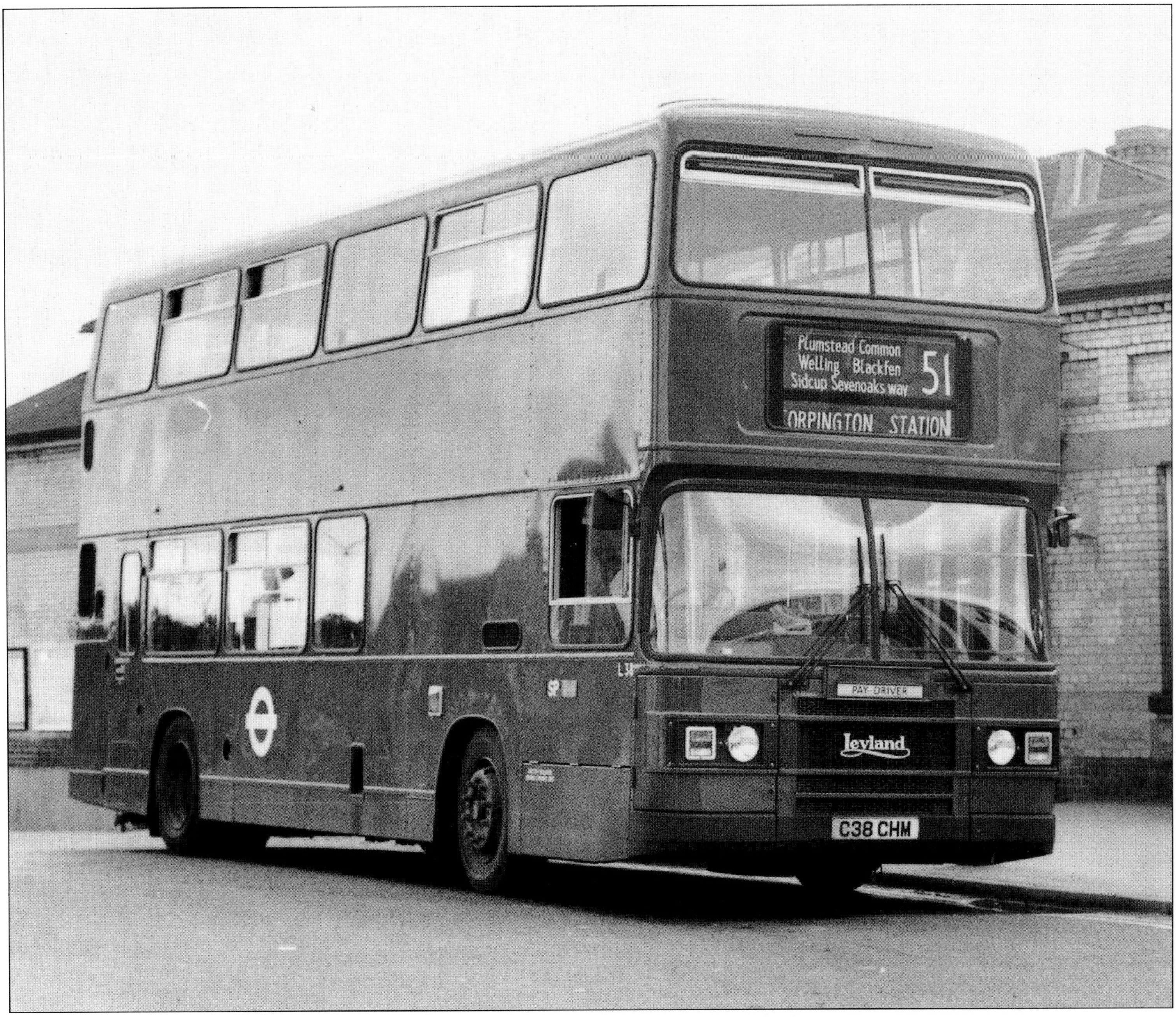

Abbreviations and Glossary

Explanation of notation used for passenger arrangements

B42F+20 standing	B = single-decker Bus, 42 seats, F = Front entrance (ie single-door), plus 20 standing
B33D+34	As above, but 33-seat, D = Dual door (ie front entrance, centre exit)
C53F	C = coach
DP43F	DP = Dual purpose single-deck bus/coach
H43/29D	H = Highbridge, ie standard double-decker, seating capacity — 43 seats upstairs over 29 seats downstairs; dual door
H32/24R	As above, but rear-entrance, open platform. (RD would denote rear entrance with platform doors.)
L27/28R	L = Lowbridge, ie double-decker with sunken side gangway on upper deck

AEC	Associated Equipment Co
AFC	Automatic Fare Collection
BEA	British European Airways
BOAC	British Overseas Airways Corporation
BRCW	Birmingham Rail & Carriage Works
DiPTAC	Disabled Persons' Transport Advisory Committee
ECW	Eastern Coach Works
ENSA	Entertainments National Services Association
GLC	Greater London Council
LBL	London Buses Ltd
LGCS	London General Country Services
LGOC	London General Omnibus Co
LPTB	London Passenger Transport Board
LRT	London Regional Transport
LTE	London Transport Executive
NBC	National Bus Company
NCME	Northern Counties Motor & Engineering
OMO	One-man operation
OPO	One-person operation
PSV	Passenger service vehicle
RLST	Round London Sightseeing Tours

Front cover:
RML 901 on the No 6 to Hackney Wick at Ludgate Hill. *Kevin Lane*

Back cover top:
D163 in Longmead Road, Tooting, at the end of its journey from Acton Green. *V. C. Jones/IAL*

Back cover bottom:
L307 passing through Isleworth on its way to Sunbury Village. *Kevin Lane*

Previous page:
L38 at Orpington station in August 1986 on a route 51 working from Woolwich. *Kevin Lane*

Below right:
RTs have long been a part of the bus preservation scene, few bus rallies having at least one representative. Indeed, it seems at times that their presence is compulsory! There were plenty on show at the RT/RF rally on 9 July 1989 at Leighton Buzzard railway station, a few miles outside of their traditional operating territory. *Kevin Lane*

First published 1997

ISBN 0 7110 2516 9

Published by Ian Allan Publishing

an imprint of Ian Allan Ltd, Terminal House, Station Approach, Shepperton, Surrey TW17 8AS.
Printed by Ian Allan Printing Ltd, at its works at Coombelands in Runnymede, England.

Code: 9705/B2

Contents

THE BATTLEFIELD
22
BLACK WHITE
HOMERTON
318c
301
AYLESBURY

Introduction

There have been many, many books written about London Transport and its buses, covering almost every aspect of their use and operation. So why yet another one? The problem with having so many different publications is that all of this information is widely dispersed and, in many cases, long out of print. Therefore with the final break-up of London Buses, I felt this was an opportune time to review the buses operated since 1933 together in one book.

The classes described are those types bought and operated over the period 1933-94, although there are some anomalies. Those types inherited by the LPTB before the war are not included; indeed these alone would make an interesting book. We start with the T and STL classes (but including those acquired within these classes), right through until the last class to be bought, the SLW class of low-floor Scanias. Odd classes acquired since the war, such as the secondhand V class Ailsas are included, however. In all cases I have attempted to give account of their lives in London, such as why they were bought, where they ran and what happened to them after withdrawal. Later chapters deal with hired buses, demonstrators and other buses to have operated on behalf of London Transport over the years, together with a few words on privatisation. It has indeed been a complex story; much more so than I realised when I began this project!

The bibliography indicates the sheer number of other sources that I referred to, and in particular the class histories published by the PSV Circle have probably proved the most useful. As with all books, this is by no means a one-man effort, and many fellow enthusiasts have come to my aid with photographs, information and suggestions. In particular I must thank John Hambley, who, as a publisher of his own London bus books, has helped with many aspects of this one. Graham Smith and David Ruddom are also thanked for their checking of the manuscript. The various photographers are each credited, some of whom have gone to the trouble of finding pictures of specific vehicles — thank you all. Maureen, my wife, is credited as always, who still doesn't object to a house that sometimes resembles a secondhand bookshop. No thanks at all are extended to my children, who always want Dad when he is in the middle of an important bit!

Kevin Lane
Dunstable,
November 1996

London Central's LD3, a Leyland Leopard PSU3E/4R formerly with Crosville Wales and acquired in 1988. Seen here at New Cross, it later returned to Wales, serving with Venture, Cardiff. *Kevin Lane Collection*

Setting the Scene

The date 1 July 1933 was a momentous one in the history of transport in London. This day saw the formation of the London Passenger Transport Board, created to operate almost all public transport in the capital. This co-ordination brought together all bus, (with one or two exceptions) tram and underground services generally within a 25-mile radius of Charing Cross, under the one administration. The seeds of amalgamation, however, had been sown years before: the London General Omnibus Company had been formed as long ago as 1856 and subsequently succeeded as the dominant bus operator in London. Over the years the company consolidated its position by buying out its competitors, or, in some cases, entering into traffic agreements.

The early 1920s witnessed a huge increase in the number of independents operating in London, which gave the LGOC much cause for concern. These were the so called 'pirates', who swarmed into the capital between 1922 and 1924 with the aim of poaching passengers from the more lucrative routes running through central London. This rash of private enterprise was severely curtailed by the 1924 London Traffic Act, the restrictions of which made the setting up of new companies a none-too-attractive prospect. Many of the new independents joined the London Public Omnibus Company in the hope of strengthening their position, but these too fell to the LGOC in 1929. The surviving operators were therefore generally well-run businesses, although the end was in sight for them also, as 1933 approached.

It may be imagined that on 1 July 1933 all buses running in London immediately became part of the LPTB, but this was far from the case — instead it turned out to be quite a protracted affair. The LPTB did take responsibility for a number of companies from day one: those that were part of the 'Underground' group of companies, including the Underground Electric Railways Company. These included the LGOC and London General Country Services and also all tram and trolleybus operations. Maidstone & District, Thames Valley and Watford Omnibus also relinquished certain services on this day. As for the rest, it had been the intention to have completed negotiations for their sale by the beginning of 1934, but in the event these discussions dragged on until the end of the year. Even then, there were a few loose ends not tied up until October 1939.

From a vehicle point of view, those inherited from the independents were, by and large, a motley lot. Alongside the highly standardised and largely AEC fleet of the LGOC, came representatives from Leyland, Dennis, Guy, Gilford, Commer, Chevrolet, Bedford, Dodge, Bean, Ford, Tilling Stevens, Saurer and Thornycroft, to name only some. Although some attempt was made to concentrate the various chassis types at particular garages, in many cases vehicles stayed close to where they had worked previously. Not surprisingly, the non-standard types were soon disposed of, replaced by new buses.

Few independents were able to buy buses built by AEC, as the company was associated with the LGOC. However, some AECs were taken in, to join the relevant class, such as LT, ST, STL or T. The bulk of the opening fleet was, of course, that supplied by the LGOC and included large numbers of NS, LT and ST types and plans were soon afoot to extend standardisation; so much so, that by the outbreak of war, most buses and coaches were of AEC manufacture, the many acquired types having been swept away by a tide of Regents and Regals. The only exceptions were some Leyland Titans of the TD class, BD class Bedfords and DA class Dennis Darts, all of which were withdrawn by the summer of 1939. As a result of Parliamentary lobbying over the loss of their London market, Leyland supplied STD, TF, CR and C classes during the 1930s. While the two main classes, the STL and T had originated before the formation of the LPTB, new designs, such as the rear-engined CR and the underfloor-engined TF were developed after 1933. All but one of the side-engined Q class were built during this time also. Although the first of a new generation of double-decker, the RT class, was to emerge in 1939-40, the war brought these developments to a halt. It was all the board could do to keep the buses running, aided by a large number of hirings and the necessary intake of non-standard buses in the shape of utility Bristols, Daimlers and Guys. The immediate postwar situation

Left:
The LPTB inherited a motley collection of vehicles, perhaps more so in the Country Area. Peoples of Ware relinquished eight routes in the Hertford area on 30 November 1933 and with them came a fleet of 20 vehicles, including a Chevrolet van. Twelve of the vehicles were Thornycrofts, some of which received fleet numbers NY1-9. NY6, UR 7353, was a 20-seat Thornycroft A2, bodied locally by Thurgood. It dated from 1930, the year that this model was discontinued. NY6 is pictured a long way from home, outside the Green Man at Longfield Hill in spring 1934, waiting to leave for Gravesend Clock Tower, on route 490. NY6, together with NY9 (UR 9176, a Thornycroft A12), passed to Collier of Abertillery in 1938, both surviving until 1950. *A. B. Cross*

Below:
The standardisation of the mid-1950s was broken by the emergence of a new class, the Routemaster. An interesting trio of buses stands on layover at Colindale station in 1958; from left to right are RTW81, RT3014 and RM1, the latter with its modified front end with which it re-entered service in March 1957. The 260 was worked by RM1 until August 1958, and thereafter was worked by the type between January 1962 and July 1984.
Kevin Lane Collection

was grim also, with a great public desire for travel coupled with a chronic shortage of serviceable buses. Hirings were again the order of the day, while new buses were delivered.

Amid all this came a change in administration. From 1 January 1948 the LPTB was replaced by the London Transport Executive, part of the nationalised British Transport Commission. Two significant events to take place during the LTE's 15-year existence were the abandonment of the trams in 1952 and of the trolleybuses 10 years later.

Although the storm clouds were gathering, in the form of staff shortages and falling passenger numbers, from a vehicle point of view the fleet entered its most standardised period. By the middle of the 1950s all prewar and wartime classes had gone: 1952 saw the last of the LTC and ST classes in service, while 1953 claimed the last B, CR, LT and TF. The last of the C and D classes were withdrawn in 1954, as were the last 10T10 Regals. Three double-deck types fell in 1955: the last Guy, G436, (the rest having gone by 1953), STD and STL. Finally, the last of the 'prewar' RTs bowed out of passenger service at Hertford in 1957. The vast majority of the double-deck fleet by then consisted of the ubiquitous RT family in its various AEC and Leyland forms, although a little variety could be experienced with the low-bridge RLHs. Besides this, the new Routemaster had appeared in its prototype form, although it would not enter service in any quantity until 1959. Single-deckers had been standardised on the RF and GS types, with only the TDs and the remaining Ts to break their monopoly.

Above:
One of the sights at Aldenham was the overhead gantry crane that carried bus bodies away for attention. A Streatham RM body is caught in midair around 1982. RM body lifts continued until 1983. *Kevin Lane Collection*

Below:
Transition at Kingston: RF369 and BL86 rub shoulders during the last month of RF operation in London, in March 1979. From a purely aesthetic point of view, the 27-year-old RF compares well with its more modern replacement. Alas, even the BL is but a memory in London service, although a number do survive as training buses. *Kevin Lane*

In order to exploit this standardisation fully, the engineering back-up had to be fully streamlined. Since 1922, the London General and LPTB had a purpose-built bus overhaul and construction works at Chiswick, and in the postwar period was looking to be too small to cope with the fleet of the 1950s — remembering that buses were about to replace the trams. A new overhaul works was developed at Aldenham, where a large maintenance facility had been built to service tube trains belonging to the Northern Line extension, plans for which had been abandoned after the war. Aldenham was used to give vehicles a complete overhaul — amounting in effect to a rebuild, while Chiswick remained open to recondition mechanical units and for other maintenance work. Aldenham was to be the largest bus overhaul works in the world, with the capacity to deal with 50 buses every week. Bodies would be separated from their chassis for attention, manoeuvred around on huge overhead gantry cranes. The two would be eventually united, although not necessarily with each other, hence the sight of old bodies on newer chassis and vice versa.

The 1956 service cuts followed by the 1958 strike saw the withdrawal of many buses, including the Craven RTs in 1956 and the 14T12 AEC Regals in 1959, while a start was also made on the sale of the Park Royal-bodied RTs and RTLs. The 1960s began with a new type, the RW class AEC Reliances, all three of them, and a flood of Routemasters, replacing the last trolleybuses in 1962. The Green Line network also benefited from the first Routemaster coaches later the same year.

From 1 January 1963 responsibility for the running of the buses passed from the BTC to the London Transport Board. Staff shortages and passenger numbers were still declining. The answer appeared to be in high capacity, one-man operated single-deck buses, as recommended in *Reshaping London's Bus Services*, published by London Transport in 1966. Many routes would be shortened, with a flat-fare system introduced. The 36ft AEC Merlin single-deckers introduced were not a success, with their poor reliability and manoeuvrability. Eventually they were superseded by the shorter 33ft 5in Swifts, were just as unreliable and both types had depressingly short lives in London. Meanwhile, the RTs, RFs and RMs soldiered on.

By the time LT had committed itself to all these single-deckers (the MB and SM families eventually totalled a little over 1,500) legislation had been passed in 1966, allowing the operation of one-man double-deckers. Experience with the two small batches of rear-engined double-deckers, the XA and XF classes, led to large orders of the DMS class of Daimler Fleetlines. Alas these were to prove to be a less-than-ideal tool for service in London, with the first one to be sold for scrap, DMS251, leaving the fleet in February 1979, six months after the delivery of the last, DM2646. Indeed, this was two months before the last of the RTs were withdrawn!

The fortunes of subsequent major classes have been rather better, with Metrobuses, Leyland Olympians and Titans all proving a success. Like many others, London turned to the Leyland National for its single-

deck requirements. The 1970s also saw minibuses, in the shape of the Ford Transit, in the fleet for the first time (although the 20-seat Leyland Cubs of 1935-6 weren't much bigger!).

The Transport (London) Act of 1969 saw the transfer of the Country Area and Green Line services to London Country Bus Services, a new subsidiary of the newly formed National Bus Company, which took effect from 1 January 1970. The Central Area buses came under the control of the Greater London Council until it was abolished in 1984. One act of the GLC was to cut fares, but this was deemed to be illegal and they were subsequently increased to a level higher than before. The decrease in passengers led to widespread service cuts and saw the withdrawal of the first Routemasters — over 200 of them were declared surplus in September 1982.

Responsibility for London's buses passed to London Regional Transport in June 1984; that body was charged with putting routes out to private tender, allowing other operators to bid for services alongside London Buses, the separate bus-operating subsidiary of LRT. The fleet was gradually changing, as the effect of this route tendering began to bite. In many areas, the mini and midibus has become the order of the day. Vehicles have often been ordered in smaller numbers for a particular contract. Although such a proliferation of different classes has not been seen since before the war (not to mention those of the independent operators also now running in London), many of these are based on the Dennis Dart chassis, which has almost become a London standard. By 1997 there were some 1,200 Darts in service in London, with an array of different body types, representing the largest number yet of single-deckers in London on the same chassis — assuming, of course, that one counts the Merlin and Swift as different chassis, which was debatable!

Events have thus, in some ways, come full-circle; the standardised mid-1950s now seem a very long way off indeed. A tenuous link between 1933 and 1994 may be observed: it is interesting to note that the last STLs were still running in 1955, when the first of the Routemasters was under trial.

In order to prepare London Buses for privatisation, 11 bus operating units were formed in 1989: Leaside Buses, London Forest, East London, Selkent, London Central, South London, London General, London United, CentreWest, Metroline and London Northern. In addition, there was also London Coaches, Stanwell Buses (Westlink) and Orpington Buses, the latter absorbed by Selkent, already operating. London Forest failed to make it to privatisation — loss of tenders and other problems saw it closing in 1991 — its remaining routes being redistributed among East London, Leaside and London Central. The stage was thus set for the privatisation of London's buses, a process completed with the sale of South London in 1995.

Above:
London Transport attained 50 years of service in July 1983, the Jubilee celebrations including a gala at Chiswick works and a rally at the London Transport Museum at Covent Garden. A number of vehicles finished in commemorative liveries during the year, one of the less well known was perhaps LS194 of Croydon garage. *Kevin Lane Collection*

Below:
Perhaps a typical London scene in the late 1980s/early 1990s, with London Buses and independents working side by side. Brent Cross in August 1991, playing host to an RI Tours Dennis Dart on the C11, a Grey-Green Volvo B10M on the 210 and several LB vehicles, SR105 and a collection of Metrobuses. *Kevin Lane*

Class T

Chassis: AEC Regal
Bodywork: See below
Numbers: T1-798
Total: 798
Dates new: 1929-32/36/38/39/46/48

The T class of AEC Regals was introduced by the LGOC in 1929-30, and these, along with a number of vehicles acquired by takeover, formed the class in the early years of the LPTB. Whilst these are strictly speaking beyond the scope of this book, a brief description of the vehicles involved would help to set the scene.

The first of the class were T1-37/39-50 and T156. All were originally fitted with petrol engines and were bodied by the LGOC at Chiswick. All had rear entrances with the exception of T156 which had the first front entrance. Excluding five buses that passed to East Surrey (an LGOC subsidiary) in 1931, all were later rebuilt to front entrance. This first batch was quite long-lived, with 18 of the survivors being rebuilt by Marshalls in 1949. These, along with eight others, were fitted with oil engines from STLs and worked at Kingston until 1953. Odd man out was T38 which carried an LGOC coach body for, eventually, Green Line service. It was sold for scrap in 1938.

T51-149/155/157-206 were 27-seat rear-entrance coaches introduced by the LGOC in 1930 and destined for the new network of Green Line routes. The bodies were built by the LGOC at Chiswick, Short Bros and Hall Lewis, each supplying 50. Most were sold in 1938-39 following the arrival of the 10T10 coaches, although a handful survived for various duties during the war. T120 had been fitted with the body off T305 in 1945 and lingered on in the Central Area, still painted green, until 1949. T150-4 were five Hoyal-bodied coaches for the LGOC private hire fleet, built in 1930 and disposed of in 1938.

T207-306 were further Green Line coaches, fitted with 30-seat front-entrance bodies by Duple (50), Ransomes (25) and Weymann (25), entering service in 193031.The arrival of the 10T10 coaches in 1938 saw their demise on Green Line duties, although many saw further service as buses (including 26 rebodied as 11T11 buses) and converted to lorries. Of this batch, T219 has been preserved.

T307-318 were 12 buses owned by LGOC but operated by Thomas Tilling, new in 1932 and worked from Bromley garage. In LPTB ownership they went to Kingston until the late 1940s. T317 outlived the rest by becoming the Chiswick Accident Demonstration Unit until 1952.

The LGOC subsidiary, Green Line Coaches Ltd, had acquired a number of vehicles from the operators they had taken over prior to July 1933 and gave numbers in the T class to the AEC Regals, an interesting collection with bodywork by Dodson, Hall Lewis, London Lorries and Strachan. These were T307-18 (later renumbered by the LPTB to T391-402, already taken by the ex-Tilling Regals), T319-24, T346-58. Those AEC Regal coaches acquired from independents by the LPTB were numbered T359-68, while numbers T369-90 were given to AEC Regal buses acquired by the LPTB.

It was not until 1936 that the Board put new AEC Regals into operation. These were the 50 vehicles of the 9T9 class of coaches for Green Line service and were numbered T403-452. Bodywork was by Weymann, seating 30, and they were easily identified by their integral bonnet and nearside wing giving a rather heavy

Below:
Representing those members of the T class acquired by the LPTB is T359. It entered service in January 1932 as a Strachan-bodied coach with Amersham and District and was acquired by the LPTB in November 1933, along with T361/2/4/5/6. All were withdrawn in 1938, having been used on Green Line work at Amersham and all except T365/6 were fitted with oil engines and Weymann bodies from R class AEC Reliances late in 1938. This early 1950s view shows T359 allocated to Uxbridge garage and laying over on route 224. Disposed of in 1953, the bus passed to the dealer North of Leeds. *V. C. Jones/IAL*

Opposite top:
T440, a 9T9 variant, now reduced to bus status, operating from Northfleet garage on route 450 in May 1951. Less than a year later London Transport disposed of it to a New Malden dealer. *V. C. Jones*

Opposite below:
A May 1939 view of 10T10 T558, just under a year after it had entered service at Dorking, where it was still allocated. The scene is Eccleston Bridge, Victoria, where T558 is arriving on Green Line route K3 from Horsham. The vehicle was exported in 1953 to serve with Sarajevo Transport, Yugoslavia. *G. H. F. Atkins*

appearance. They were somewhat underpowered, having 7.7 litre oil engines, but nevertheless enabled the disposal of many acquired coaches. Their Green Line duties continued until the summer of 1939. At the outbreak of the war the 9T9s were put onto bus work. Replaced by 10T10s and TFs, they were all converted to public ambulances and allocated to certain Central Area garages. This use continued for the duration, except for T414-6/21/22/43 loaned to the US Army during 1942-46. After the war, the 9T9s rarely returned to Green Line duties, being relegated to bus work, mainly in the Country Area but also on Central routes from Uxbridge and Hornchurch garages. The class bowed out of service during 1952-3. T448, which passed to Harperbury Hospital, St Albans, on withdrawal, survived long enough to be preserved.

The next sub-class was the 10T10 type, T453-718, more Green Line coaches, which flooded the network during 1938-39. These carried Chiswick-built bodies seating 30 or 34 and were an improvement on the 9T9s, being powered by 8.8 litre engines. The widespread introduction of the type inevitably saw the demise of most other acquired coaches. As with the 9T9s, they were withdrawn on the outbreak of war and were converted into public ambulances, although most had been put back into passenger use by the end of the year. The events of 1940 saw a number of reconversions however; many were later used by the US Army, including the well-known 'Clubmobiles', mobile canteens used by the American Red Cross, and named after US states and cities. Most of the class resumed Green Line duties in 1946, but were replaced in time by the RFs. Many were relegated to bus duties, with 40 being actually converted as such and painted red, then put to work in the Central Area. A few were also used on the BEA service to Heathrow Airport, both in Green Line and Central Area guise.

Withdrawals came thick and fast from 1953 as the RFs came into the fleet. The last Central Area 10T10s ran from Kingston in May 1953, while those in the Country Area bowed out in July 1953, the last running from Dorking, Dunton Green, Northfleet, Staines and Hitchin. Thereafter, a few lingered on as spare or relief vehicles, although the last ones survived as staff buses for Chiswick works until 1957. Around a third of the 10T10s were sold for export, while the rest ended up mainly in non-PSV use. T504 has been preserved, having survived plans to convert it to a showroom in 1954 and a mobile crane in 1959.

The last prewar sub-class was the 11T11 variant, created in

1938 by the fitting of 1935 Weymann 30-seat bodies to earlier coach chassis which were also re-engined with new 7.7-litre oil units. The bodies had previously adorned former LGCS R class AEC Reliances, themselves rebodied from their Chiswick originals. These 31 went to the Country Area, although 22 were later transferred to the Central Area. All were disposed of during 1952-53.

After the war, two further variants were introduced: the 14T12 and 15T13. The former consisted of T719-768, Weymann-bodied buses for Central Area use and were operated from Uxbridge, Kingston, Muswell Hill, Sidcup and Hanwell garages, being delivered during 1946. They were gradually replaced between 1955 and 1958, most being exported to Ceylon.

The 15T13 class were AEC Regal IIIs and carried Mann Egerton bus bodies. Numbered T769-798, they entered service in the Country Area, initially at Hemel Hempstead and Watford, in 1948. In 1956-57, 12 were transferred to the Central Area, seeing service at Kingston and Norbiton, still in green livery. These workings lasted until September 1959, although two remained at Tring and Crawley until 1962. Two lingered on as staff buses until the following year. Most went to Ceylon as well, although T792 has been preserved.

Above
A 1953 view of Weymann-bodied T746, allocated to Kingston garage and seen working on a 201 journey towards Hampton Court station. This bus was amongst the last batch to be disposed of, to the Ceylon Transport Board in 1958-9. *John Hambley Collection*

Left:
T787, one of the 30 Mann Egerton-bodied 15T13s put into service in 1948, photographed amid RTs at Crawley garage in September 1960. Latterly used as a staff bus, it was the last of the class and was not disposed of until August 1962, ending up with a Mansfield contractor. *Tony Wild*

Class STL

Chassis: AEC Regent
Bodywork: LGOC/LPTB/ Tilling/Park Royal/ Birch/Weymann
Numbers: STL1-130/153-2681
Total: 2,659
Dates new: 1932-39/41/42/46

Left:
The three-window arrangement on STL125 identifies its Tilling origins. New in June 1933 to London General, it was among the batch STL51-130 operated by Thomas Tilling and ordered to replace the last open-top Tilling-Stevens. The bus is seen in Lower Gravel Road, on a 61 journey from Bromley during the late 1940s; it was withdrawn in June 1949 and sold for scrap.
V. C. Jones/IAL

Below:
STL166, seen here at Chessington Zoo in August 1949, was also new in June 1933 to London General. Its first garage was Hendon, although by 1949 it was allocated to Turnham Green, from where it was finally withdrawn and replaced by RTs a month after the picture was taken.
V. C. Jones/IAL

The STL was the standard London double-deck bus of the 1930s. It was designed by the LGOC to supersede the ST (short type) following the increase in the permitted length of a four-wheeled double-deck bus in 1932, the classification being an acronym of Short Type Lengthened. The first batch of 50 entered service from January 1933 and were AEC Regents with Chiswick-built LPTB H34/26R bodies. They were fitted with petrol engines and crash gearboxes, except for STL50 which had a pre-selective gearbox. All were initially allocated to Clayhall garage. They duly passed to the LPTB in July 1933, mostly surviving the war to be withdrawn over the period 1947-50. The exceptions were STL2/11/13/26/32, all scrapped following an enemy raid at Croydon garage in May 1941. After withdrawal none saw further passenger service, although STL9/12/24/38/42/43 were converted to lorries for the service fleet.

STL51-130 were built for the LGOC but operated on its behalf by Thomas Tilling. The first of these entered service in October 1932, thus pre-dating the first of the LGOC buses. The LPTB took over the Tilling operations in London whilst production of this batch and the last 22, which would have been STL131-152, were cancelled. Their bodies were built by Tilling and were distinguished by having three windows at the front on the upper deck. They began life at Bromley, Catford and Croydon and in common with the London General batch were petrol-engined with crash gearboxes. Normal withdrawals saw the bulk of them sold for scrap during 1947-50, STL59/75 ending their days with standard Chiswick-built bodies. In May 1941, 22 of the Tilling STLs were lost to enemy action at Croydon, while another, STL63, went the same way at Elmers End in July 1944.

The second batch of STLs for London General were numbered STL153-202, with delivery beginning in June 1933. In July and August of that year 25 of these were delivered new to the LPTB. Bodywork and petrol engines were similar to those fitted to the first batch. Four were destroyed at Croydon in May 1941; the rest survived until 1947-49. Twelve were converted to lorries, with three of these still existing in preservation.

Six further acquired AEC Regents were fitted into the STL class. STL553-7 were from the fleet of Charles Pickup, acquired in November 1933 and carrying Park Royal open-top bodies, subsequently fitted with roofs. STL558 came from the Redline fleet in December 1933 and carried a Birch body from an earlier Daimler CF6. Of the Pickup STLs, 554 was destroyed at Croydon in May 1941, the others being scrapped after the war. STL558 was luckier, being rebodied as a coach for G. & S. Motors, Hooton, in 1947.

STL203-552/559-608 carried a more modern looking LGOC-designed body, seating four less than those fitted previously, the reduction taking place on the upper deck and resulting in a H30/26R arrangement. Petrol engines were fitted, in most cases using secondhand units from LT class buses converted to oil, to all of this batch, with the exception of STL342-52, which were oil from the start. Many of the petrol engines were subsequently replaced by oil during 1939. This large batch of vehicles took to the streets between August 1933 and November 1934, going to Central Area garages, ousting LT, NS and some

Left:
STL490, carrying the redesigned Chiswick-built body as originally fitted to STL203-608, was new in July 1934 and lasted until June 1952. This late 1950 picture sees it passing a fine line of taxis at Golders Green, on a 226 to Cricklewood. *V. C. Jones/IAL*

Below:
The 410, Bromley North-Reigate, received 12 'Godstone' STLs in 1934; they stayed for 16 years, replaced by new RLHs in 1950. STL1055 looks in fine fettle in this postwar view. This particular vehicle may have been the longest-lived, surviving with a couple of Yorkshire operators until 1955. *John Hambley Collection*

Bottom:
A total of 89 front-entrance STLs were ordered for the Country Area and delivered during 1935, allowing the removal of a variety of older types. Here STL1058 leaves Windsor for Slough, although by the time of its withdrawal in 1953, it was allocated to Reigate. *V. C. Jones/IAL*

Opposite top:
STL1875 is one of the 'tunnel' STLs, as can be seen by its modified roof profile. Interestingly these buses were also fitted with reinforced tyres which were required because of the way they rubbed against the kerb inside the Blackwall Tunnel. These buses, allocated to Athol Street garage, were finally ousted by RTLs in 1953. *V. C. Jones/IAL*

acquired types. By the time that they were withdrawn, between 1947 and 1954, some were allocated to Country Area garages. A total of 22 were lost through enemy action at Croydon in 1941. Many of them were sold for scrap, particularly the earlier ones, although a number did see further use both at home and abroad. STL441/469 have been preserved, while STL390 is preserved as a breakdown tender, into which it was converted in 1949.

Amid these deliveries came a dozen lowbridge AEC Regents, initially not numbered, but which became STL1044-55. New in April/May 1934, they had been ordered by London General Country Services. 8.8 litre oil engines were fitted in view of their need for hill climbing and front-entrance bodywork was supplied by Weymann, seating 26 over 22. These were the famed 'Godstone' STLs and were allocated to Godstone and Reigate for route 410 which encountered a low bridge at Oxted. When they were displaced from here in 1950, they went to Guildford and Addlestone following a period in store. Most were withdrawn in 1952, although STL1051-3/5 saw some use during the Coronation in 1953.

STLs were now entering the fleet in great numbers, with rapid modernisation taking place. For instance, in 1933 there were 2,149 of the NS type in stock. All had been taken out of passenger service by the end of November 1937. By September 1939, STL2647 had been reached, but there had been much variety within their ranks. STL2014-2188 were fitted with Park Royal bodies, similar to the Chiswick product but built with metal frames. Forty buses from the batch STL1809-1884 had bodies with curved roofs in order to negotiate Rotherhithe and Blackwall tunnels on routes 82 and 108. An interesting experiment was performed on STL857 in 1935 when it was fitted with a full-width cab, sharply sloped to the top deck giving an attractive streamlined appearance. It ran in this form until 1938, numbered STF1. STL1260-3 were special short-wheelbase chassis on which were mounted one Dodson and three ST bodies which had formerly sat on four Daimler CH6 chassis.

Most of the STL intake was destined for the Central Area, although STL959-1043/1056-9 and 1464-1513 were built for the Country Area and had front-entrance bodies by Chiswick and Weymann. Thirty nine buses from the STL2516-2647 batch delivered in 1939 were allocated to the Country Area,

being the first rear-entrance STLs for this area. Unlike the 'Godstone' STLs, these were all to highbridge layout.

The only STLs to be built during the war were STL2648-81, new in 1941-42. Bodywork was an assortment of new and secondhand, these buses being finished in wartime red, but being allocated to the Country Area. Chiswick also built 20 lowbridge STL bodies, delivered in 1942/43, and mounted on a variety of chassis in for overhaul at that time. Other wartime activities included pay-as-you-enter experiments, which included the rebuilding of STL1793 and 2284 in 1944-45.

In 1950 withdrawn STL2477 was relicensed and received an experimental body with removable body panels, allowing easy replacement in the case of an accident. It was known as the Sainsbury body, after its designer, Arthur Sainsbury, although others dubbed it the 'Meccano Set'.

One further batch of STLs was built: Weymann-bodied STL2682-2701. These entered service at the beginning of 1946 and were of provincial appearance, quite different from all other STLs. All were sent to the Country Area, allocated to Watford and Luton for routes 321/351. These were destined to be London's final STLs, the last running at Hertford at the end of May 1955. All found homes with municipal operators: Dundee took 10, Grimsby six and Widnes four.

Above:
The final STLs had a provincial air about them, because of their very non-London looking Weymann bodies. STL2699 waits at Uxbridge before leaving for St Albans in June 1949, when just over three years old. Withdrawn in 1955, STL2699 was one of the 10 to be bought by Dundee Corporation. STL2692, one of those that were sold to Grimsby Corporation, survived to be preserved. *V. C. Jones/IAL*

Below:
Chiswick-bodied STL1684 was one that survived a little longer after disposal by London Transport. After serving as a trainer at Watford garage for almost two years it was sold in 1954, serving as a mobile furniture showroom in London until 1961 when it was sold for scrap. *Kevin Lane Collection*

The rest of the STLs were gradually withdrawn over the period 1947-54, replaced by the flood of RT types during this period. The last Central Area STLs ran on route 101 out of Upton Park garage at the end of June 1954, while those in the Country Area clung on a bit longer, until the end of August. Half of the 24 that made it to the end were transfers from the Central Area and still in red livery. Many went for scrap, worn out after wartime service, although others saw further passenger or non-PSV service; 160 became the basis for the SRT class, a stopgap measure as described later.

Class Q

Chassis: AEC Q
Bodywork: LGOC/Metro-Cammell/Weymann/BRCW/Park Royal
Numbers: Q1-238
Total: 238
Dates new: 1932/4-7

The AEC Q type has often been described as revolutionary, and indeed it was. The design, which took the engine away from the time-honoured position at the front and put it along the offside, was an experiment by AEC, which designed and built the prototype at its Southall works in 1932. The placing of the engine behind the front axle allowed better accessibility and less intrusion into the saloon. The resulting vehicle, which carried a full-fronted 37-seat body built by the LGOC, presented a startlingly modern appearance.

The bus was registered GX 5395 and entered service with the LGOC in September 1932 on route 11E from Shepherds Bush to Liverpool Street from Hammersmith garage. It was numbered Q1 by the LGOC, the letter Q apparently referring to secret naval craft of the first war and applied to the bus, reflecting its 'hush-hush' nature. The bus duly passed to the LPTB where it became a Country Area vehicle, classified 1Q1, and was used on both Green Line and bus duties from Reigate. It was withdrawn and sold to a dealer in 1946, ending its days as a chicken house in Norfolk in the 1950s, a sad end for such an historic vehicle.

The next four members of the Q class were perhaps even more impressive, double-deckers built for Central (Q2/3) and Country (Q4/5) duties.

Q2/3, registered AYV 615/6, carried Metro-Cammell 56-seat bodies, with entrances placed ahead of the front wheel. As with Q1, power was provided by AEC six-cylinder petrol engines. They were classified 2Q2 by the LPTB. Although entering service at Harrow Weald in July 1934, by July 1937 they had been transferred to the Country Area at Leatherhead, and later Hertford. They were stored during the war, Q3 suffering damage during an air raid at Elmers End in June 1941 and subsequently dismantled. Q2 was sold to a dealer in 1946 and later rebodied as a single-deck coach body. By 1951, however, the bus had become a mobile snack-bar.

Q4/5, classified 3Q3 and registered BPG 507 and BPJ 224 respectively, went into service in August 1934 and were always Country Area buses, operating initially from Leatherhead and Hertford garages. These two were easily distinguished from Q2/3 by the air-operating sliding doors, positioned centrally. Bodywork was by Weymann, again seating 56, but later reduced to 53. Both buses were stored from 1940, being disposed of in 1946. Q4 served with Blue Ensign, Doncaster, for several years, while Q5 went even further north to join the fleet of Garelochhead Coach Services, later becoming a caravan.

Experience with the single-deck Q1 resulted in the delivery of a large batch of further Qs for the Country Area during 1935-36. Classified 4Q4, they were fitted with oil engines and numbered Q6-105/186/7, a total of 102 vehicles. Bodywork this time was by the Birmingham Carriage & Wagon Co and initially seated 37, although this was soon reduced to 35 by replacing the two seats across from the driver with a bulkhead, and further still down to 32 during the war, although these three seats were later restored. They were spread out around the Country Area, with the largest allocations going to the two Watford garages, replacing former London General Country Services' ADCs in the main. There was some change of status before the war, with 27 becoming Green Line coaches in 1937, part of this batch having previously seen use in the Central Area first. All except one were returned to Country Area bus work in 1938, and as such continued on these duties until the RFs came along in 1953-54, although a few were transferred to the Central Area again after the war, principally at West Green and Kingston.

Disposal of the 4Q4s began early in 1952 and continued for two

Left:
Q103 was one of the 27 4Q4s converted for Green Line service in 1937. It is seen on Eccleston Bridge, Victoria, in September 1937 working route A2, Gravesend-Sunningdale, from Northfleet garage. Prior to this, Q103 had been one of a small number of the type to be painted red and used on route 226 from Cricklewood during 1936-7. It reverted to bus duties in the following August, being withdrawn in 1953 and later exported to Malta. *G. H. F. Atkins*

Below:
Q157, a Merton-allocated 5Q5, passing Wimbledon station working on a 200 journey between Wimbledon and West Wimbledon around 1950. *V. C. Jones/IAL*

years. Many saw non-PSV use, with contractors and showmen, while 10 went for export to Malta, Cyprus and Libya. Three 4Q4s were preserved: Q55 was retained by London Transport, while both Q69 and 83 have survived through their use as transport for the elderly, at Gravesend and Sutton Coldfield. Q75 passed to the London Transport service fleet in 1952 for civil defence duties, latterly numbered 1035CD, although still retaining its Q prefix on the vehicle itself. It went to a dealer in 1964.

Q106-185, classified 5Q5, were Central Area single-deckers, although of a shorter wheelbase than the 4Q4s with the entrance positioned ahead of, rather than behind, the front wheels. Bodywork was by Park Royal, seating 37; all were delivered during 1936. As it turned out, only 53 started life as red buses as the other 27 went to the Country Area to take the place of the 4Q4s converted to Green Line coaches, these only gradually gaining red livery between 1938 and 1949. They became the oldest Central Area single-deckers by the time of their withdrawal in 1953-54. The entire class of 5Q5s passed to the dealer W. North of Leeds, most of which saw no further use, although a few were exported to Libya, Malta, Cyprus and Burma.

The last Q class single-deckers were the 50 Green Line coaches, Class 6Q6 Q189-238, which went into service in 1936-37. Fitted with 32-seat Park Royal bodywork the entrance was placed behind the front wheel. Their use as coaches was curtailed by the war, when all were converted to public ambulances, joining AEC Regals (9T9 and 10T10 types) and TF class Leylands on these duties. All except Q217 (destroyed at Elmers End in 1944) returned to Green Line work after the war. The influx of RFs saw their storage in 1951-52, although 24 of the better ones were put onto Central routes 210/244 at Muswell Hill, still in green livery, between March and October 1952, replacing elderly LT class AEC Renowns. All except for a couple went to North's, and of these only a couple of non-PSVs and several exports appear to have seen further use.

The gap between the 5Q5 and 6Q6 classes was filled by the unique Q188, classified 7Q7. It was a double-deck, six-wheel coach fitted with a Park Royal 51-seat body and was delivered early in 1937; a handsome machine indeed. It had been intended to operate the vehicle on Green Line service from Romford, but union opposition saw these plans shelved. Q188 was rather under-powered for such duties, with only a 7.7 litre petrol engine at the driver's disposal. Following a time in store, Q188 was banished to Hertford and put onto bus work on route 310, where the other double-deck Qs ended up. Stored again during the war, Q188 operated for Brown, Garelochhead, following disposal in 1946 and was later converted to a lorry for the conveyance of furniture, which was apparently not successful and it was subsequently scrapped.

Above:
6Q6 Q203 on Green Line route 715, Guildford-Hertford, passing through Enfield in October 1950. This was one of the class to be briefly reinstated, at Muswell Hill in 1952. *R. E. Vincent*

Below:
An official AEC photograph of Metro-Cammell-bodied Q2. Despite the blind display for the 77, it entered service, along with Q3, from Harrow Weald on route 114 from July 1934, passing on to Middle Row for use on route 52 at the beginning of 1935. In July 1937 the pair were transferred to the Country Area. *AEC*

Bottom:
Former Q9 and Q73 passed to Carlyle (Contractors). Q9 is seen during its service there between 1954 and 1956; it would end up as scrap in 1957. *J. A. Senior*

Class C

Chassis: Leyland Cub KP3, KPO3, SKPZ2
Bodywork: LPTB/Short/Weymann/Park Royal
Numbers: C1-98/106-13
Total: 106
Dates new: 1934-36

An early task for the LPTB was to find a suitable vehicle to replace the many and various smaller inherited buses. A Leyland Cub KP3 chassis was examined early in 1934 and this led to the purchase of one later that year. It received a Chiswick-built 20-seat body and became C1, registered AYV 717, the first of the class. The vehicle was of normal control and was powered by a Leyland six-cylinder petrol engine, although this was later removed in favour of a Perkins four-cylinder oil engine. C1 entered service in the Central Area in October 1934, initially from Hounslow on the 237, but later from Merton and Barking, before being transferred to the Country Area a year later.

The first batch of Cubs, C2-75 (BXD 631/27-29/32/30/33-700), was allocated to the Country Area during 1935, replacing the motley collection of small buses acquired from independents. These were of Type KPO3, powered by Leyland six-cylinder oil engines, and carried 20-seat bodies built by Short's of Rochester, similar to that built at Chiswick. C51 went to the Central Area at Barking in November 1935 and stayed in the Central area until withdrawal in 1944. A number of the class was transferred to the Central Area during the war, while C16/52/69 were loaned to other operators during this period.

The next batch was 22 for the Central Area. C77-98 (CLE 105-126) were put into service in April and May 1936, mainly to enable the withdrawal of the former LGOC Dennis Darts in use in the suburbs. These were similar to the first batch but with Weymann bodywork and a slightly more powerful Leyland engine, and were put to work initially at Harrow Weald, Enfield, Hanwell, Mortlake and Barking. Six of this batch were loaned to Edwards of Lydbrook during the war, while many of them ended their days in the Country Area; some were repainted green.

The odd man out of the Cubs was C76, a KP3 model acquired with St Albans and District in November 1933 and was useful in evaluating the type before placing big orders. It was registered JH 2401 and carried a 20-seat body of unknown make.

The withdrawal and disposal of these normal-control Cubs was quite protracted. C1 was taken out of service early in the war, turning up with a couple of London independents during the late 1940s. The Country Area batch (C2-75) were mostly withdrawn in 1953-54, many being exported to Ceylon. Earlier disposals at the end of the war saw 21 sent over to Belgium via the Belgian Economic Mission. Of the Central Area batch, C77-98, nine went to Belgium, the rest passing largely into non-PSV use, although C94 has been preserved. C76 was withdrawn from Windsor, some way from its earlier haunts, in October 1938.

Above:
C1 was withdrawn in November 1940, although not disposed of until 1946. It served with a couple of London coach operators, including J. M. Coaches, Holloway, with whom it is seen here on hire to London Transport working on route 19, Finsbury Park-Clapham Junction. *V. C. Jones/IAL*

The final batch of Cubs was rather different from the others. C106-113 were forward-control SKPZ2 models and had six-cylinder petrol engines. They were bought for use on the inter-station service which connected the main railway termini, and carried 20-seat Park Royal single-deck bodies, with the passengers sitting above space for luggage. A blue and cream livery was applied. They began work from Old Kent Road garage in October

1936 and remained on these duties until 1942 when they were repainted khaki and saw use with ENSA carrying entertainers around the country. Their inter-station duties were resumed from 1946 until replacement by RTs in 1950. They were finally hired to British European Airways from Gillingham Street for a period during 1951.

Following disposal, a notable new owner for C107 and C111 was the London Fire Brigade; they were used as a control unit and personnel carrier respectively, the latter subsequently passing into preservation on its withdrawal in 1961.

It will be noted that there is a gap between the numbers of the last two batches of vehicles. C99-105 were allocated to Leyland SKZ1 lorries, while C114 was a catering van on a similar chassis, all new in 1936 for the service fleet.

Above:
Short-bodied C50 after arrival at Hertford on a 388 journey from Mardley Hill in August 1952. C50 was to remain allocated to Hertford until withdrawn in November 1953. It later passed to a Sussex farmer, along with C36 and C53, late of Dunton Green, surviving into the 1960s. *A. B. Cross*

Below:
Inter-station Cub C112 awaits customers at Victoria in April 1950, operating from Old Kent Road garage. These Cubs were replaced on this duty in the November by ordinary RTs. Sadly their attractive light blue and cream livery was not continued on the double-deckers. After a period on hire to BEA the class was disposed of, C112 ending up as a henhouse in Perthshire. *A. B. Cross*

Class LTC

Chassis: AEC Renown
Bodywork: Weymann
Numbers: LTC1-24
Total: 24
Dates new: 1937-38

Early in 1937, consideration was given to the replacement of the private hire fleet of AEC Regals dating from 1930-31 and inherited from London General, East Surrey and Lewis Omnibus of Watford. The vehicles subsequently chosen were a fleet of 24 six-wheeled AEC Renowns, the last of this model to be built, with Weymann coachwork. They formed the LTC class, numbered LTC1-24 and registered EGO 505-528, entering the fleet in 1937-38 from Brixton and Old Kent Road. Before entering service, the vehicles were fitted with reconditioned petrol engines from LT class double-deckers. The first 14 carried seating for 28, but were soon increased to 30, while the other 10 were 30-seaters from new. All 24 coaches were ready for the 1938 season, ousting 18 T class AEC Regals, DST6, a former West London Coaches Daimler CH6 and an Albion.

With the outbreak of war in September the following year, the whole LTC class were among those coaches almost immediately converted into ambulances for public use, and adapted to carry eight stretchers. The vehicles were put on stand-by at various Central and Country garages and were not converted back to coaches until the end of 1945.

Their postwar life was varied, with private hire duties, Green Line and even bus work undertaken, such was the shortage of vehicles at times. I doubt whether many passengers complained about the luxury offered! In 1949-50 the entire class was re-engined with oil units taken from STLs, while withdrawals took place in 1951-52, the vehicles being replaced by private hire RFs and RFWs. All passed to dealers and oblivion, no examples apparently seeing further service.

Below:
LTC2c in its wartime role as a public ambulance allocated to Chalk Farm garage. Note, however, that it has neither masked headlamps nor white-painted mudguards, so perhaps this view was taken soon after conversion. *John Hambley Collection*

Bottom:
LTC21 working out the last few months of its life as a bus, here allocated to Chelverton Road, Putney, on route 30, Hackney Wick-Roehampton. The LTCs were withdrawn in two batches; 18 went in October 1951, including LTC21, the remaining six following a year later. *John Hambley Collection*

Class STD

Chassis: Leyland Titan TD4, TD4c, TD7, PD1
Bodywork: Leyland/ Park Royal
Numbers: STD1-176
Total: 176
Dates new: 1937/41/42/46

In 1937 the LPTB placed into service the first 100 of the STD class, Leyland Titan TD4s with Leyland bodywork, numbered STD1-100 and registered DLU 311-410. These buses represented the only double-deckers to be bought new by the Board before the war not to be built by AEC. The first 90 of these were more-or-less standard Leyland TD4s, with certain special features, such as having AEC steering gear. They were fitted with standard four-speed constant mesh gearboxes and Leyland six-cylinder oil engines. The other 10, STD91-100, were of the TD4c type: that is having standard Lysholm-Smith type torque-converter transmission, also known as the 'gearless bus' type. However, while these buses gave a smoother and quieter ride, use of the torque-converters increased fuel consumption to such a level that they were removed at their first overhaul during 1939.

The Leyland bodywork fitted to STD1-100 was similar to those on contemporary STLs, including roofbox, and seated 56 (the last 10 were 55-seaters until the torque-converters were removed).

All 100 STDs were allocated to Hendon garage, entering service between April and July 1937 and replacing NS, ST and STL types on routes 13, 16 (Sundays), 28, 52, 83, 113 and 183. Throughout their lives, this first batch of STDs became synonymous with Hendon. A number went to Enfield in 1952 to replace G class Guy Arabs on routes 107 and 107A, being withdrawn from there.

These prewar STDs were withdrawn from passenger service during 1953-54, although a few lingered on as training buses into 1955. Most passed to dealer W. North Ltd of Leeds and subsequently turned up with a variety of owners, several ending up converted into lorries. None survived to be preserved.

The second batch of STDs were 11 'unfrozen' Leyland TD7s obtained from the Ministry of Supply during the war and fitted with Park Royal austerity 56-seat bodies. These TD7s were similar to the TD4s but were to a slightly shorter wheelbase and did not include any particular London features. STD101 entered service at the end of 1941 (carrying, incidentally, the prototype double-deck austerity body) with the rest trickling into use during 1942. All worked from Gillingham Street garage, Victoria, throughout their lives, although complaints from staff and passengers saw their demise in 1951, some surviving as training vehicles for a little longer. Again, most went to W. North of Leeds.

An additional 65 STDs entered the fleet after the war to aid the replacement of older vehicles, before RT production had resumed. STD112-176 were again all-Leyland vehicles, although by now the current chassis was the PD1. In order to speed up deliveries, the chassis were the standard product with almost no special London features. The bodywork did contain some London alterations — a roofbox was again fitted — but oddly there was no rear destination display, only a stencil route numberplate in the platform window.

All entered service during the last few months of 1946, initially at Potters Bar, Gillingham Street, Loughton, Hanwell and Croydon, but later also from Leyton and Stockwell garages. The demise of the postwar STD was swift, with all members of the class finding themselves redundant following severe service cuts implemented from February 1955. Loughton operated the last on the 28th of that month. All of the class are believed to have been subsequently exported to Yugoslavia.

Below:
All-Leyland STD1, working from Hendon on a Pinner-bound 183, a typical duty. The location is Golders Green station around 1950. STD1 was withdrawn in November 1953, passing initially to Yuille, Larkhall, before ending up at the dealer North of Leeds.
V. C. Jones/IAL

Top:
The severe lines of Park Royal-bodied STD109, one of the utility STDs, seen on a 137 at Clapham Common in June 1950, some eight months before withdrawal. *V. C. Jones/IAL*

Above:
STD154 of the postwar batch at Leytonstone in April 1947, parked in front of an LT class six-wheeler. The STD was just five months old, one of 17 initially allocated to Loughton garage. It was withdrawn from there in March 1955. *V. C. Jones/IAL*

Class TF

Chassis: Leyland Tiger FEC
Bodywork: LPTB/ Park Royal
Numbers: TF1-88
Total: 88
Dates new: 1937/39

The TF class, following on from the Q, was another attempt to improve on the engine position, in this case, horizontally-mounted on the offside, under the floor. The vehicle was built in conjunction with Leyland and designated Tiger FEC. The power unit was a modified Leyland 8.6 litre oil engine, while the body was a 34-seat coach built at Chiswick. TF1 was registered DYL 904 and entered Green Line service in December 1937, initially at Tunbridge Wells. As built, TF1 sported a distinctive cab with much use of glass in its construction which made it look rather like the cockpit of an aircraft. This was rebuilt to resemble the rest of the class in 1940. Withdrawal came in 1943 and in 1946 it was sold to Castle Coaches, Lewisham.

The first batch of vehicles were for the private hire fleet; numbered TF2-13 they were registered as FJJ 603-14, arriving during April, May and June 1939.

Bodywork was supplied by Park Royal, seating 33, and the whole batch was allocated to Old Kent Road garage. All except TF9 were lost during the bombing of Bull Yard, Peckham, in October 1940, while the survivor lasted with London Transport until 1952.

TF14-88 were Green Line coaches, entering service between March and September 1939 and were registered FJJ 615-18/629-674/761-77 and FXT 41-48.

The bodywork, seating 34, was built at Chiswick this time and all were initially allocated to Romford, London Road garage. Events, however, overtook them, and all were converted to ambulances for use in the Central Area during the war. The class was converted back to coaches from late 1945 and most were ready for the recommencement of Green Line services which began in 1946. The influx of RFs saw the downgrading of most of the class to bus work in 1952 and final withdrawal by the following year.

Most of the class passed to North, the Leeds dealer, and several were later converted to lorries. TF77 was the one chosen for preservation by London Transport.

Below:
TF9, the only member of the private hire batch to survive the war, is seen working from Gillingham Street garage at Beaconsfield in May 1951. It was withdrawn a year later, went to the dealer North of Leeds and was possibly later exported.
V. C. Jones/IAL

Overleaf top:
Green Line TF36 seen in the early postwar years, working the half-hourly route 720 to Bishop's Stortford. Seen departing under the trolleybus wires from Aldgate, this particular bus had been reconverted from an ambulance in November 1947 and was downgraded to bus work in May 1952, being withdrawn from Hatfield garage in September 1952. It subsequently ended up with the dealer North of Leeds. *V. C. Jones/IAL*

Overleaf bottom:
TF26, which latterly worked from St Albans garage, also went to North's, although it was later used as student transport in London, W1. It was subsequently owned by contractors in Hampshire and Wiltshire in 1957-8, but it was with a dealer for part of 1958, which is presumably where this view was taken, surrounded by surplus military equipment. *Kevin Lane Collection*

GREEN 720 LINE
BISHOPS STORTFORD
FJJ 647

FJJ 637

Class CR

Chassis: Leyland Cub REC
Bodywork: LPTB
Numbers: CR1-49
Total: 49
Dates new: 1938/39

In an attempt to improve on the conventional engine position, London Transport and Leyland Motors had collaborated to design the underfloor-engined TF class as previously described. At the beginning of 1938 came another experiment, this time with the engine appearing at the back, together with the gearbox and radiator. The first rear-engined Cub went into service in January 1938 and was fitted with the same power unit as the conventional Country Area Cubs. The Chiswick-built body was in some respects similar to that of the TFs, although the overall effect was rather neater. CR1 was registered ELP 294 and was used initially from St Albans, moving to Streatham following storage during the war years.

An additional 59 vehicles were subsequently ordered, but their number was later reduced to 48. CR2-49 were registered FXT 108-155 and were delivered from the outbreak of the war. The engine used was the more powerful 4.7 litre unit as fitted to the conventional Central Area Cubs, while the bodywork was similar to that on CR1, but included a number of detail differences. The intention was to put the class to work on one-man Central Area duties, but the war curtailed these plans. However, initial allocations included Kingston, Hounslow and Uxbridge during 1939-40, although some were stored, including CR36/40/42/44/45 which did not enter service until 1946. Six of the class (CR12-17) were painted green and served at Windsor, where they were joined by CR1.

After the war, the class — less CR18 which was destroyed along with all but one of the private-hire batch of TFs at Bull Yard, Peckham, in October 1940 — was used mainly on relief duties. Most of them were withdrawn during 1949, the last five survivors being replaced by GSs in 1953, the very last running at Swanley in the November. Most went to dealers, although several are known to have been sold abroad, and CR16/36 at least, have been bought for preservation from Cyprus, to join CR14, which was retained by London Transport, and later sold into private preservation.

Below:
Merton-allocated CR6 seen on route 88 in Longmead Road, Tooting, in April 1949, just a month away from withdrawal. This bus was one of nine involved in a fire while stored at Walthamstow (Forest Road) Works, and subsequently rebuilt in 1946. CR6 ended up at North's yard in Leeds by 1955.
V. C. Jones/IAL

Class RT

Chassis:: AEC Regent 0661
Bodywork: LPTB
Numbers: RT1-151
Total: 151
Dates new: 1939/40

From the mid-1930s the LPTB and AEC had been developing a new double-deck design which would eventually replace the then standard type, the STL, which was appearing in many different variants, and other smaller classes. This new type was the RT, the first chassis of which appeared on the streets of London in 1938 beneath the Dodson body of withdrawn ex-City Leyland Titan TD118 and given the bonnet number ST1140 and registration EYK 396. It saw service at Hanwell garage on route 18C.

This new chassis featured a redesigned gearbox, airbrakes and a more powerful engine, a six-cylinder 9.6 litre, than that used on the STL. It was positioned lower down thus allowing the driver better visibility than before. After its period of service it received a new Chiswick-built body in June 1939. Seating 55 (reduced from 56 due to weight problems) it presented a modern, stylish image. Its four-bay layout gave a brighter interior and it featured a more spacious platform and staircase area, while the cab received a sliding door and other improvements. Following previous practice, a roofbox was fitted, not only at the front but at the rear also. RT1 entered service from Chelverton Road, Putney, on route 22 on 9 August 1939, less than a month before the outbreak of war.

RT delivery commenced from October 1939, with 150 further chassis arriving until May 1940. A change in body construction was made, with wooden framing rather than the metal used on that of RT1. This reduction in

weight allowed the seating to be increased to 56. The registration numbers of RT2-151 were FXT 177-326. Early allocation was to Chelverton Road on the 22 and later to Victoria and Putney Bridge. Availability was poor early on due to braking problems.

In July 1944 RT97 was damaged in an air raid and as a result was rebuilt for pay-as-you-enter experiments, appearing on route 65. In 1949 it was further rebuilt, emerging as RTC1, a Green Line coach featuring a redesigned front end. After the war, RT19 received improvements to form the basis of a new, highly standardised postwar bus, as the RT was to become.

After the war the prewar RTs continued until 1955, when severe service cuts ousted the type from the Central Area, the last running from Chelverton Road and New Cross, to be replaced by postwar RTs. A number passed into the training fleet, while others were disposed of. More interesting, however, were RT36/62/79/93/114/128 and 137, repainted green for use in the Country Area at Hertford on route 327 over a bridge that prevented the use of later RTs which were some 15cwt heavier. They continued until the rebuilding of the bridge in August 1957, when they too became training and staff buses. Several of this batch have been preserved, including the body of RT1, latterly on RT1420 as a replacement for its own Craven body. Sadly the futuristic looking RTC1 was sold in 1955 to Merseyside where it survived a further five years as a staff bus on Merseyside.

Left top:
RT19 was used by AEC as a demonstrator during the earlier part of the war. It is seen here in September 1940 working for Nottingham Corporation, complete with the AEC triangle in the roofbox. *G. H. F. Atkins*

Left below:
The unmistakable RTC1 in Green Line guise, passing Lambeth Palace in 1949. *V. C. Jones/IAL*

Above:
RT90 working from Putney, Chelverton Road, garage, on route 74 towards the end of its life in passenger service. The type was replaced at Chelverton Road by RTLs in May 1955. *Kevin Lane Collection*

Class B

Chassis: Bristol K5G, K6A
Bodywork: Park Royal/ Duple
Numbers: B1-29
Total: 29
Dates new: 1942/45-6

The disruption of the supply of new buses during the war, limited by the fact that the Ministry of War Transport designated which manufacturers could build buses, saw many operators buying anything that they could get their hands on, London included. With RT production grinding to a halt in 1940 and only a handful of STLs appearing during 1941-42 it was left to Bristol, Guy, Leyland and Daimler to supply the LPTB with new double-deckers during this period.

Bristol was one of the manufacturers allowed by the Government to supply 'unfrozen' chassis — that is, those built from parts already in stock — to operators with the most need. The Bristol K5G was a design that dated back to 1937 and it was on this chassis that the first nine of the B class were built. These were numbered B1-9, registered FXT 419-27, entering service in May and June 1942. When new, they were fitted with Gardner 5LW oil engines which were changed for AEC 7.7 litre six-cylinder units in 1948-49. Park Royal 56-seat utility bodywork was fitted and the whole batch began work from Hanwell, replacing STLs on route 97.

The class spent all of their time in London at Hanwell, with the exception of a few that were loaned to Alperton for a period. Withdrawals took place between 1951 and 1953, and all except one passed to Crosville. The exception, B5, although intended for Crosville was delivered to Hartlepool Corporation Transport after overhaul by United Automobile Services. This was also the only one to retain its utility body, the others receiving new bodies from Strachan and ECW. None survived.

A second batch of the class, B10-29, was delivered after the war, entering service in 1945-46. These were Bristol K6A models fitted with AEC 7.7 litre six-cylinder engines and carried Duple 56-seat bodies of a 'relaxed utility' design, not so austere in appearance. The lower bonnet and PV2 type radiator increased driver visibility and resulted in a more modern looking vehicle. This second batch were registered HGC 235-254.

As with the earlier members of the B class, all of these later Bristols spent their lives at Hanwell garage, with some also being loaned to Alperton. B10-29 were taken out of service alongside B1-9, the last surviving only a couple of months later, in April 1953. Needless to say, these youthful buses soon found new homes in Tilling fleets; five passed to Brighton, Hove and District, six to Crosville and seven to Lincolnshire Road Car. The other two ended up at Hartlepool, although apparently destined for Lincolnshire.

Top:
Park Royal-bodied B2 entered service in May 1942 and is seen in the late 1940s working route 97 (Greenford-Brentford) at Ealing Broadway, a regular haunt. Withdrawn in 1952, it passed to Crosville, who had it rebodied twice, by Strachan and ECW, before it was sold for scrap in 1960. *V. C. Jones/IAL*

Left:
The Duple bodies on the second batch of Bristols were less austere than those built by Park Royal. This is former B25, seen with Lincolnshire Road Car in 1956, having passed to them in 1953 along with former B10/11/15/20/21 and 26. All were withdrawn in 1960; B25 ended its days as a mobile fish and chip shop near Skegness in the mid-1960s. *Kevin Lane Collection*

Class G

Chassis: Guy Arab I/ Guy Arab II
Bodywork: Park Royal/ Weymann/Duple/NCME/ Massey/Guy
Numbers: G1-436
Total: 436
Dates new: 1942-1946/1950

The third type of utility bus to be introduced by the LPTB, and by far the most numerous, was the 436-strong class of Guy Arabs, following on from the B and STD classes. The prewar Guy model had been the Arab; the first chosen for wartime production being the Arab I, these accounting for the first 71 delivered to London.

G1-31 were Gardner 5LW-powered Guy Arab Is carrying Park Royal 56-seat utility bodies, entering service between December 1942 and July 1943. G30 was rebodied in 1944 with a similar Northern Coachbuilders utility body, running for a couple of years with wooden slatted seats. Initial allocations were to Tottenham and Hanwell garages.

G32-50 were similar to the above, but carried Weymann utility bodywork (except for G43 which was Duple-bodied). Furthermore, they shared the same duties as the first batch at Tottenham and Hanwell, being delivered over the same period.

The last of the Arab Is, G51-71, carried Park Royal utility bodywork and entered service in June and July 1943 alongside G1-50.

The Guy Arab II differed in that the chassis was longer in order to accommodate the larger 6LW engine if needed. London chose to stay with the 5LW, as did most other operators of the type. G72-136, entering service between July 1943 and April 1944, carried Park Royal utility bodies with wooden slatted seats (previous bodies, with the exception of rebodied G30, had leather seats). In addition to Tottenham and Hanwell, vehicles from this batch also went initially to Alperton and Barking garages. The first new Guys to enter service in 1945 were G137/8 with Weymann utility bodies at Alperton, to be followed by Park Royal-bodied G139-53 and NCME-bodied G154-73, entering service during the summer of 1945. These were put to work at Alperton, Barking and Gillingham Street garages, the war being over by this time.

The year 1945 also saw the arrival of several batches of Massey-bodied Guy Arab IIs: G174-193/258-268/312-318/358-368 entered service between the May and September; Park Royal-bodied G194-218 arrived in the August to October; while more NCME-bodied examples were G219-25 and G269-311, the last 11 of which entered service in 1946. Also arriving in 1945/46 were Park Royal-bodied G319-357 and Weymann-bodied G369-430 and G431-5.

Although specifications of these utility vehicles were generally similar, the various bodybuilders could be differentiated, the large front dome of the NCME-bodied examples being among the more obvious. Paint schemes were quite variable too towards the end of the war, with buses appearing in various shades of red or brown.

Below:
Park Royal-bodied G1 leaves Golders Green for Chingford, probably in the late 1940s. This bus was the first of the batch to be withdrawn — in November 1950 — from when it operated as a driver trainer until July 1951. It was sold for scrap during the following month. *V. C. Jones/IAL*

The last member of the class was G436, which was not a utility vehicle at all. Put into service at the beginning of 1950, G436 was the new postwar model, the Arab III, and was powered by a 6-cylinder Meadows engine. A Guy-built body to a Park Royal design H30/26R body was fitted, giving the bus a slightly RT flavour. Hopes that the Guy might become a London standard were not to be, the bus remaining unique. It worked from Old Kent Road, Nunhead and latterly Enfield.

The Guys performed yeoman work during the late war and early postwar period, but were unloved by crews and passengers alike. Of the utilities, the Guys were the most basic and plans to dispose of them were put in hand as soon as possible, rather than have

Left:
The extended position of the radiator of G316 identifies it as an Arab II model. This vehicle carries a Massey body and was new in August 1945. G316 was photographed in Barking in 1948 working from Rainham on the 87 route. Withdrawal came in March 1951 and it later operated with Western SMT and Alexander (Fife) with a new NCME lowbridge body and the registration FSD 459, surviving until 1968.
V. C. Jones/IAL

Left below:
The unique G436 with Guy-built, Park Royal-designed body seen in 1951 operating on route 173 (Peckham circular-Nunhead). On withdrawal in 1955 it was sold for export, probably to Yugoslavia. *V. C. Jones/IAL*

Right:
Many of the London Guys that went north to Scotland were subsequently rebuilt and reregistered. Highland K95-100 (LSC 96-101) were rebuilt and entered service in 1954, carrying Scottish Omnibuses C35F bodies, although their former identities are not known. K98 is seen in Inverness in the early 1960s. It passed to a showman following withdrawal by Highland in 1963.
V. C. Jones/IAL

Below:
Quite a number of the class ended up in Scotland. G281, one of the postwar deliveries, passed to Western SMT in 1953 and thence in 1957 to Highland Omnibuses where it was numbered E30. Seen here inside Wick garage during the early 1960s, it was sold for scrap in 1966, still carrying its original NCME utility body.
Kevin Lane Collection

them rebodied as other operators were doing. Withdrawals began late in 1950, continuing until December 1952 when Upton Park lost them on the 101. This left just G436 which soldiered on at Enfield until February 1955.

The majority of the Guys saw further passenger service, often rebuilt and rebodied by their new owners. Many went north to Scotland — to Edinburgh, Highland and Western SMT in particular — while a number were exported to Yugoslavia, Southern Rhodesia and Kenya amongst other countries. G351 is preserved, after serving over 13 years with Burton Corporation.

Class D

Chassis: Daimler CWA6, CWD6
Bodywork: Duple/ Brush/Park/Royal
Numbers: D1-281
Total: 281
Dates new: 1944-46

The final utility buses to be bought by London Transport were of Daimler manufacture. The Daimler factory had been badly damaged during the air raids on Coventry with wartime production not resuming until 1943. All of the vehicles to serve with London Transport as their D class were of the CW type, developed from the prewar COG5 chassis.

The first of the class were CWA6 type, fitted with AEC 7.7 litre six-cylinder engines. D1-6 were fitted with Duple lowbridge L27/28R bodies to utility specifications and were put into service at Merton in May and June 1944 on route 127, which included a height restriction at Worcester Park. Here they replaced lowbridge ST and STL types until the RLH class in turn replaced them from 1952. D7-34 were also fitted with Duple bodies, but of the more usual highbridge type, seating 56, and were allocated to Merton between August and October 1944.

The next batch, D35-73, carried Brush 56-seat bodies and again went to Merton during the first half of 1945. D67-69 and D71/3 were temporarily placed into Green Line service as recounted below. Further Duple-bodied CWA6s were D74-92 at Merton between March and June 1945, with Brush-bodied D93-126 arriving at Merton during the summer of 1945. D127 also carried a Brush body but was powered by a Daimler 8.25 litre six-cylinder engine and was thus designated CWD6. This was, however, later replaced by an AEC power unit.

The next four buses were again of the lowbridge type, CWA6s with Duple bodies. D128-31 went to Merton to join D1-6 on the 127 at the end of 1945, to oust the remaining lowbridge STLs.

December 1945 to March 1946 saw the entry into service of a large Duple-bodied batch, D132-181. Of these 12 were of the CWD6 type but built to an improved design, although like D127, AEC engines were later substituted. The bodies on the CWA6 examples were less austere than those built earlier, being in the 'relaxed utility' style. A number of these were put straight to work on Green Line duties from the reopened Romford (London Road) garage in March 1946, while these were joined by D67-9 and D71/3 in 1948. All were subsequently repainted red working from Merton after their replacement by new Green Line RT3224-59 in 1950.

Despite the ending of the war, further Daimlers were purchased for fleet renewal, the last 100, D182-281, arriving between May and November 1946. These were all of the CWA6 type and carried Park Royal 'relaxed utility' style. For once, these were not destined for service at Merton; all of them being to Sutton where they were used on all routes.

With the reallocation of the Green Line Daimlers in 1951 following a period of de-licence, the entire class was now at either Merton or Sutton garages. However, the poor condition of the bodies saw the first withdrawals taking place in 1952 and the last in 1954, when Sutton's D226/250 and Merton's D73 ran for the last time on 8 January.

The Daimlers found a ready market, with Belfast Corporation taking 97 and Southend Corporation 13. Some 23 passed to Leeds independent Samuel Ledgard, while 83 went overseas to Ceylon. Many of these were rebodied and gave many further years of service. Others went to a variety of operators, with the original bodies still fit for service. Southend's D27, rebodied by Massey, and Belfast's D93, rebodied by Harkness, have been preserved.

Left:
Brush-bodied D52 waits at Leatherhead in 1951, about to work on route 65 as far as Chessington Zoo. To the right is RTL563, which will later travel the entire length of the route to Ealing. D52 was one of the last of the class to be withdrawn, in January 1954, joining 12 others with Southend Corporation and was subsequently fitted with new Massey bodywork. *V. C. Jones/IAL*

Above:
D163 has a Duple body and is making a sharp right-hand turn to avoid parked cars in Longmead Road, Tooting, at the end of its journey from Acton Green, around 1950. D163 survived until October 1953 to become one of many Daimlers to be sold to Belfast Corporation and receive new Harkness bodywork. In this form it ran until 1970. *V. C. Jones/IAL*

Right:
Ninety-seven Daimlers were bought by Belfast Corporation and rebodied by Harkness; 486 and 520 are seen here in June 1964, being formerly London Transport D140 and D142 respectively. Both were withdrawn six years later. *Mike Sutcliffe*

Class TD

Chassis: Leyland Tiger PS1
Bodywork: Weymann/ Mann Egerton
Numbers: TD1-131
Total: 131
Dates new: 1946-49

In the immediate postwar period there was an urgent need to replace ageing prewar rolling stock. London had turned to Leyland to ease the double-deck shortage with further STDs in 1946, and also bought single-deckers from the same source in the shape of the TDs, standard PS1 chassis with Weymann and Mann Egerton bus bodywork.

The first batch of Leyland PS1s, TD1-31, were registered HGF 959-989 and entered service between December 1946 and March 1947. These carried Weymann 33-seat front-entrance bodies and were put to work at Muswell Hill, mainly on the 212 route, until replaced by new RFs in 1953. Most of the batch subsequently moved to Kingston with a few going to Loughton, although they all ended up at the former. In 1954 their seating was reduced by one to allow more circulating room. They were withdrawn from Kingston during 1956-58, TD17 being the last one in service. The majority of the first batch were exported to Ceylon, although five followed the postwar STDs to Yugoslavia.

A second batch of TDs were put into service during 1948-49, again to alleviate the prevailing vehicle shortage. These were numbered TD32-131 and registered JXC 225-324. The chassis were the same as that of the earlier batch, but the bodies were built by Mann Egerton of Norwich. These were similar to those bodies built for T796-98 except that, as these were ordered for the Central Area, no sliding door was fitted, although there was provision to fit one. This feature also set them apart from the Weymann bodies, other differences including half-drop rather than sliding windows and a straight line underneath the destination box at the front, that of TD1-31 being curved. These bodies were originally 31-seaters, but were reduced by one during 1954 in a similar fashion to the first batch.

TD32-131 were used to replace early T class AEC Regals and LT class AEC Renowns at Hornchurch, Enfield, Hanwell, Kingston, Harrow Weald, Muswell Hill, Edgware, Leyton and Tottenham and later also worked from Loughton, North Street, Norbiton, Uxbridge and very briefly at Plumstead, where they ran for a couple of months on new route 256 until replaced by RTLs.

The TDs were themselves gradually replaced between 1958 and 1962, largely by RFs, but also by RTs in a few cases. Although the majority of these ended up at Kingston, the last one, TD124, ran from Edgware on the 240A in October 1962. A batch was required here to pass beneath the bridge at Mill Hill Broadway station. A number of this batch were also exported to Ceylon, but many ended their days with mainly non-PSV owners in this country. TD95 and 130 have been preserved.

Below:
TD20, one of the Weymann-bodied batch, stands at Muswell Hill Broadway in 1953, waiting to leave on a 244 working to Winchmore Hill. The whole of this batch was allocated to Muswell Hill garage from new although they were to be displaced by RFs from 1953. TD20 was exported to Ceylon in 1958. *John Hambley Collection*

Above:
Kingston in the late 1950s with Mann Egerton-bodied TD35, TD106 behind, working to Staines. TD35 was withdrawn in July 1959 and was one of many to pass subsequently to the Ceylon Transport Board. *Kevin Lane Collection*

Right:
Mann Egerton-bodied TD104 stands outside Edgware garage, all set for duties on the 240A, the last route on which this class operated,until October 1962. TD104 survived until then, subsequently passing into non-PSV use in south London. *Kevin Lane Collection*

Class Postwar RT

Chassis: AEC Regent III
Bodywork: Craven/Park Royal/Saunders/Weymann
Numbers: RT152-4825
Total: 4,674
Dates new: 1947-54

As the war was drawing to a close, work was beginning on an updated version of the prewar RT design. The requirement was for a bus to replace not only the STs, STLs, LTs and wartime utilities, but the trams also. RT19 was used for this development work, improvements on the chassis and engine being incorporated in the new design. It was later fitted with the body from RT1, whose chassis had been dismantled. The new body, like that formerly on RT1, was to be of all-metal construction. It was similar in appearance to the Chiswick product, but included many detail differences, such as a squared-off cab window and an altered destination display. The roof number box was retained at the front but that at the rear was removed. These bodies were designated RT3 and were built by Weymann and Park Royal, seating 56. They were built to the same standard design to allow complete interchangeability.

May 1947 saw the entry into service of the first Weymann-bodied member of the class, RT402, on the 10th, and Park Royal-bodied RT152 appeared on the 23rd: both operated from Leyton garage and were rather more modern than the open-staircase LT class vehicles they replaced!

RT production proceeded with 171 licensed in 1947, rising to 900 by the following year. There were problems in the supply of bodies because of a shortage of materials and skilled labour. AEC had to resort to storing a number of chassis. Because of this, tenders were invited to construct bodies, bringing Saunders and Cravens into the story. At its factory in Beaumaris on Anglesey, Saunders built bodies for RT1152-1401 and 4218-67, which were compatible with the other RT3 bodies. Those built by Cravens at Sheffield definitely were not, being finished to a different profile and having five rather than four lower-deck windows. Cravens built only 120, for RT1402-1521. Although a decision to abandon the roofbox had been made in 1946, due to their being prone to damage by low trees, particularly in the County Area, the changes could not be implemented until many bodies had been built. Thus all Craven and Saunders bodies had them, as did around 700 Park Royal and 600 Weymann bodies. The later, non-roofbox bodies were classified variously RT8 and RT10.

The numbers of RTs available for service increased steadily, with 1,639 licensed in 1949; 2,765 in 1950; culminating in a peak of 4,553 in 1954. (These figures do not include prewar RTs nor

Below:
Green Weymann-bodied RT1046 went into service in December 1948 at Leatherhead. It is seen here at Chessington Zoo in August 1949, still looking quite smart. *V. C. Jones/IAL*

Top right:
A line-up of Saunders-bodied RTs waiting to leave Anglesey for London. RT1298 leads 1297 and 1299, together with a number of others. RT1297/99 entered service at Leyton in January 1950, while RT1298 went to Holloway during the same month. *Saunders-Roe Ltd*

Bottom right:
RT3224-59, also Weymann-bodied, were new in August 1950 and were allocated to Romford for Green Line duties, replacing D class Daimlers. Although they were finished in all-over Lincoln green livery with raised metal 'Green Line' bullseyes on the sides, they were otherwise ordinary RTs. Here RT3249 waits at Aldgate on a 722 working to Dartford, via the Dartford Tunnel, which had opened in November 1963, the 722 being extended from Upminster, Corbets Tey accordingly. These Green Line RTs were replaced by new RCLs during the summer of 1965. *V. C. Jones/IAL*

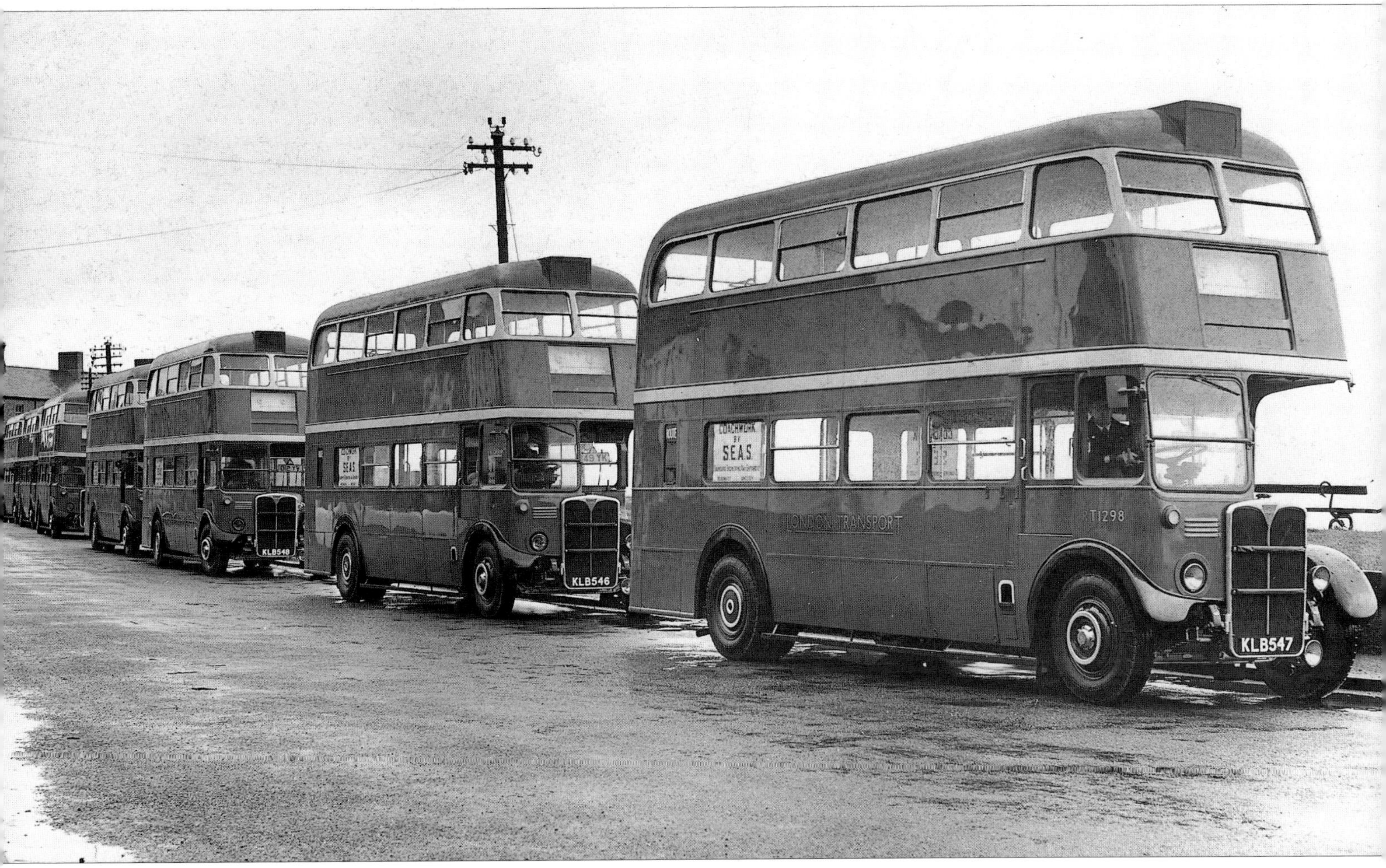
COACHWORK BY
SEAS
LONDON TRANSPORT
T1298
KLB547
KLB546
KLB548

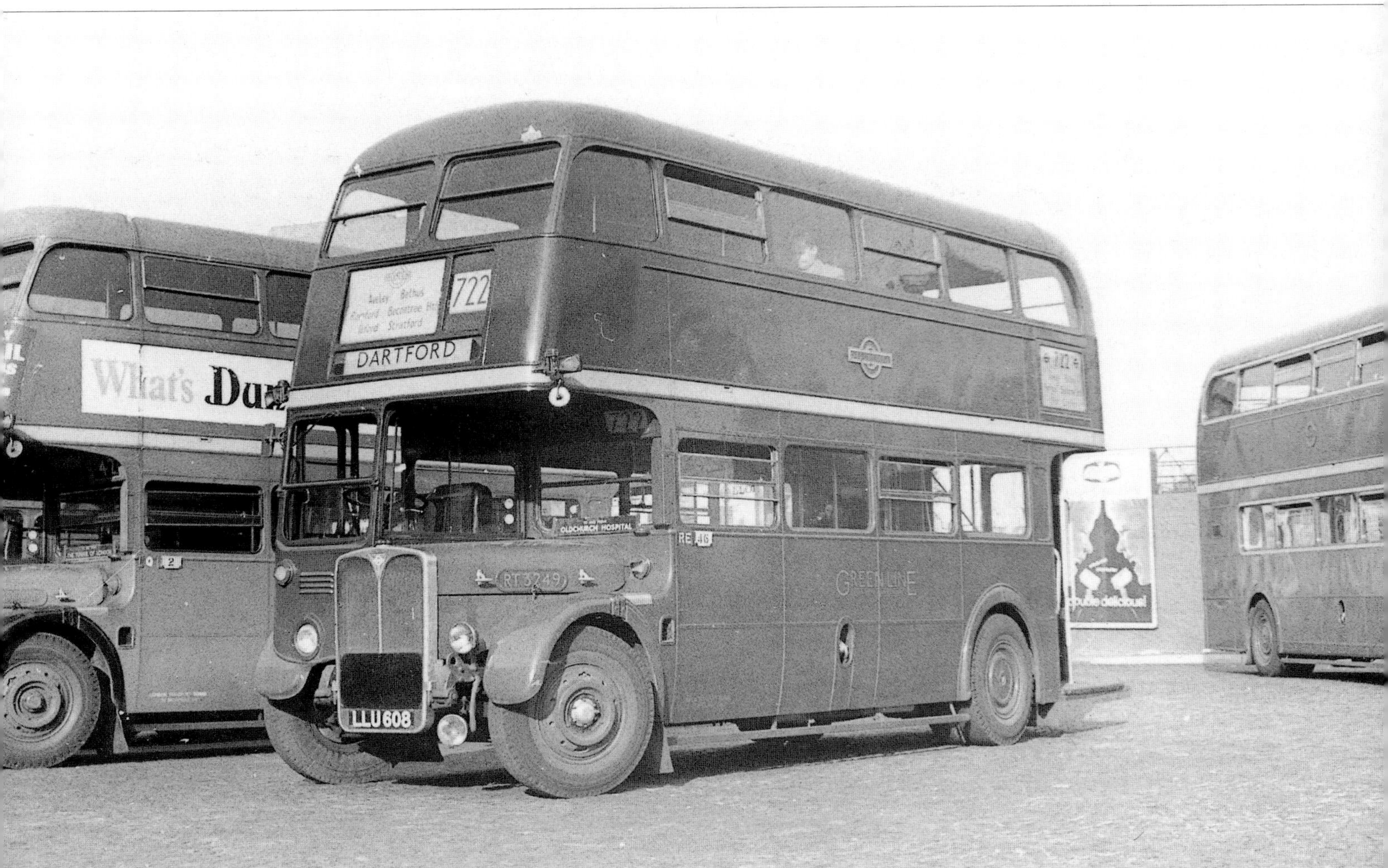
722
DARTFORD
What's
RT3249
GREEN LINE
OLDCHURCH HOSPITAL
RE 46
LLU 608

Above:
The overhaul procedure at Aldenham, whereby chassis and body part company, meant that older bodies often turned up on more modern chassis. This is illustrated here by RT4721, new in March 1954, carrying an early roofbox RT3 body. *Kevin Lane Collection*

Right:
Nearly the end; Plumstead's RT192 on a Saturday 122 journey to Slade Green station, loads at Crystal Palace in 1977. The 122 lost RTs in favour of RMs in April of the following year, with the Saturday-only extension from Bexleyheath garage and Slade Green station being withdrawn at the same time in the first phase of 'Busplan 78'. RT192 was withdrawn itself and sold for scrap later in 1977. *Kevin Lane Collection*

Opposite top:
Although London Transport had finished with driver training RTs by the end of 1979, London Country used them until March 1981. RT4496, complete with dented front dome, looks decidedly shabby outside Windsor garage in January 1980. Not surprisingly, RT4496 was withdrawn later in the year, passing to a private buyer. *Kevin Lane*

Opposite below
The non-standard Craven-bodied RTs were the first to be withdrawn, being disposed of by Bird's Commercial Motors of Stratford-upon-Avon during 1956. One recipient was Staffordshire independent, Beckett of Bucknall, which took former RT1405/7/13/30/32/47/49/58/68. Three years earlier, Beckett had also bought former STL504/1599, although both were acquired for spares only. RT1413 is seen outside Beckett's premises in the early 1960s. PMT bought Beckett's business in March 1965, all except RT1405 passing to the new owners. The other eight were soon disposed of, RT1413 ending up in a Barnsley scrapyard. *Kevin Lane Collection*

RTL/RTW types.) The highest number reached was Park Royal-bodied RT4825, which entered service in March 1954 at Cricklewood. By this time, however, there was a surplus of RTs (and RTLs), and a number were stored before entering service. The honours for the last RT to enter service fell to RT4773, taking up its duties at Northfleet in August 1959. By this time, earlier members of the class had already been withdrawn, including the entire Craven-bodied batch, sold for disposal to Bird's Commercial Motors, Stratford-upon-Avon in 1956. Furthermore, 50 standard RTs were deemed surplus in 1958, these (together with 100 RTLs) also going to Bird's. Of these 50, half went to Bradford City Transport. 1958 also marked the beginning of the great exodus of RTs to Ceylon; it would last for 10 years and in all 266 RTs made the journey, together with 279 RTWs and 728 RTLs.

The overhaul procedure at Aldenham, the works float system, was introduced in 1955, resulted in early bodies appearing on later chassis and vice versa. Thus, roofbox RT3 bodies would appear with suspiciously high bonnet numbers.

Although the majority of RTs were intended for bus work, a few were earmarked specifically for Green Line duties. In 1950, RT3224-59 were allocated to Romford, London Road for use on services to Aldgate. They were finished in Lincoln green

livery with a raised Green Line roundel on the between-decks panels, no external advertisements being carried. For all their pretensions, however, they were more or less ordinary RT buses. Similarly, RT4489-4509 were allocated to Grays in 1954 to replace lower-capacity RFs on route 723. Standard Country RTs were of course often to be seen on Green Line reliefs and could be seen well into the 1970s.

RTs began to be replaced by Routemasters from 1962, once the trolleybus conversion had been completed. A notable landmark was the last roofbox bus to be withdrawn from service: RT1903 in March 1971. A total of 484 RTs passed to London Country Bus Services in 1970, although such was the shortage of buses that 34 were sold back to London Transport in September 1972. This shortage also prolonged the lives of many others, recertified for

Above:
Apart from those RTs that went to the scrapyard, the majority probably ended up in non-PSV use. Lesney, the manufacturers of Matchbox toys, employed many as staff transport at their various factories — and in such a capacity former RT4399 waits at the Rochford factory, near Southend, to leave for Canvey, in May 1983. It is heading a line-up of mainly ex-Eastern Counties Bristol FLFs, a type soon to replace the RTs on this duty. *Kevin Lane*

either one or three years. The mid-1970s also saw RTs allocated to many garages to cover Routemaster shortages. Although the rate of withdrawal had slowed, it picked up again during 1977. The numbers of RTs licensed for service at the end of 1973 stood at 1,097, while four years later it was only 234, and by the end of 1978 the total was a mere 13, although many more were in use as driver trainers. An interesting event during 1978 was the hiring of preserved RTs for training purposes, including Craven-bodied RTs and RTLs.

By the beginning of 1979, only route 62, and some journeys on the otherwise RM-operated 87, remained in the hands of RTs working from Barking garage. The RTs had been retained because of a narrow bridge at Chadwell Heath, reminiscent of the STL/RT situation at Hertford in 1957. The 62 and 87 became full RM routes from 7 April. The RTs were given a suitable send-off, with a parade of vehicles, headed by RT1, covering most of route 62. The last RTs in service earlier in the day were RT624, 1798, 2541, 2671, 3251 and 4633, with RT624 being the last one actually to run in passenger service. The last RT in service with London Country was RT604 which lasted at Chelsham until June 1978; it would have survived longer but for engine failure. The last driver trainer, RT1018, was finally withdrawn in 1981, sporting full NBC livery, which looked rather incongruous on such an elderly vehicle.

Many RTs saw further use in all types of operation, both at home and abroad. The Ceylon RTs have been mentioned; other countries to take RTs in quantity included South Africa, while many have turned up in Europe and the United States as sightseeing and tourist buses. A number of RTs undertook promotional tours to Europe, America and Canada in the early 1950s. At home in the 1960s there were RTs all over the place, rather like the DMSs were in the 1980s. Their role call is long, including such well-known names as A1 Services, Barton, Bradford, Dundee, Red Rover and Stevensons of Uttoxeter. Many more passed to smaller independents and non-PSV concerns, although an awful lot ended up as scrap with Wombwell Diesels, the Barnsley dealer.

The preservation movement has also claimed a fair number of postwar RTs, beginning with RT191, which was saved with RT44 in 1963. Since then, over 100 have survived in various states of repair, with few bus rallies taking place without at least one, while others still see occasional PSV use.

Class RTL

Chassis: Leyland Titan PD2/1
Bodywork: Park Royal/ MetroCammell/Weymann
Numbers: RTL1-1631
Total: 1,631
Dates new: 1948-54

In 1946, even before the first of the postwar RTs had been built, it was realised that AEC alone would be unable to meet the need for new buses, not only for the replacement of life-expired vehicles, but also for the trams. In view of its association with London Transport before the war, Leyland was an obvious choice as an additional manufacturer. Two types were ordered, to be classified RTL and RTW – the RTL 7ft 6in wide based on the PD2/1 chassis, and the RTW 8ft wide based on the PD2/3 chassis. The RTLs were powered by Leyland's own 9.8 litre engine, although AEC transmission was employed. The initial RTL order was for 1,000 vehicles to be bodied by Metro-Cammell, although because of many difficulties they only bodied 450, the balance going to Park Royal. The Metro-Cammell bodies were known as the RT7 type but were not interchangeable with the RT3s.

The first RTL was numbered RTL501, the original intention being to number all of the Leylands into one series, with the 8ft-wide vehicles becoming 1-500. However, it was later decided to classify these as RTWs, and commence the RTLs at 1.

RTL501 was licensed in June 1948, carrying the Park Royal body and registration (JXC 20) intended for RT657. Thus it was the only RTL to carry a roofbox from new. The first of the Metro-Cammell-bodied batch, RTL551, went into service at Tottenham in August 1949. RTL550, the last of the Park Royal batch, went into service at Camberwell in July 1950, some nine months before the last Metro-Cammell, RTL1000. Leyland received further orders for the RTL, which by 1954 had reached RTL1631. All were bodied by Park Royal with the exception of RTL1307 and 1601-31, which carried bodywork by Weymann. A number of RTLs (and RTs also) built in 1954 were not immediately required for service and were put into store. After RTL1337 had entered service at Clay Hall in October 1954, the rest of the class from RTL 1568 onwards, remained in store until February and March 1958 when 61 went into service.

All RTLs were initially destined for the Central Area, although 18 members of the class were painted green and from September 1960 were allocated to Hatfield garage, where they lasted for a year, although not particularly liked by their drivers. There were, of course, also instances of red RTLs finding themselves on loan to the Country Area from time to time.

As noted above, the only RTL to sport a roofbox from new was RTL501. However, it was inevitable that the interchangeability between the Park Royal bodies on RTLs and the Park Royal, Saunders and Weymann bodies on RTs would lead to roofboxes appearing on RTLs. In 1964 old RT3-type bodies were deliberately placed onto RTL chassis, some 23 appearing during that year.

RTLs have operated from most Central Area garages over the years, although for maintenance reasons it made sense to concentrate like with like, which meant that AEC and Leyland types found themselves at particular garages.

The first disposal of RTLs actually took place before the last to be built had been taken out of store, 50 being sold to Bird's

Below:
An early view of RTL42, operating from its first garage — Wood Green — where RTL34-50/61-68 were allocated in January 1949. The location is unmistakably that of Victoria. *V. C. Jones/IAL*

Commercial Motors, who had earlier taken the Craven RTs, in January 1958. They were eagerly snapped up by various independent operators, including Laurie (Chieftain) of Hamilton, who took 17. 1958 also saw the first of the enormous quantity of RTLs sold for further use in Ceylon, 728 members of the class finding their way there up until the end of 1968. A further 102 RTLs were exported to Cape Town during the mid-1960s. Nearer to home were the 14 sold in 1959, 1965 and 1967 to Jersey Motor Transport, and the many independents such as Barton, Red Rover, OK Motors, and A1, Ardrossan. Even Walsall Corporation took a few. A number went abroad as tourist buses and around 20 are preserved.

Left top:
The highest-numbered RTLs, 1475-1631 had 'OLD' registration numbers. OLD 859 was RTL1630, one of the RTLs which were put into store and did not enter service until March 1958 (at Middle Row). This early 1960s view sees RTL1630 working a 159 journey from West Hampstead to Kennington. *Kevin Lane Collection*

Left below:
A number of RTLs acquired earlier roofbox bodies following overhaul at Aldenham, mostly during 1964. RTL172 of Battersea garage, lays over on route 22. *Kevin Lane Collection*

Above:
Green RTL1265 on route 303 at Stevenage in 1961, during the class's short spell with the Country Area. *Alan Mortimer*

Below:
Jersey Motor Transport bought eight RTLs in 1959, followed by a further three in both 1965 and 1967. RTL411 became JMT No 3, registered J 8774 and arrived with the 1959 batch. It is seen here at St Helier in August 1969. Withdrawal came in November 1974, passing along with several others to the dealer E. H. Brakell. It later travelled to Singapore, together with former RTLs 460 and 1505, where all three were eventually submerged under the sea and used as fish farms! *Kevin Lane Collection*

Class RTW

Chassis: Leyland Titan PD2/3
Bodywork: Leyland
Numbers: RTW1-500
Total: 500
Dates new: 1949-50

The 8ft-wide RTW class was ordered with the initial batch of RTLs as already recounted. In common with the RTLs, the RTWs were Leyland products with many features specified by London Transport. The bodywork, classified RT6, was adapted from Leyland's standard structure, there being no interchangeability with those supplied by Park Royal, Weymann or Metro-Cammell due to their width. The 500 vehicles in the batch were all delivered by the end of 1950, the first, RTW1, having entered service back in May 1949 from Tottenham on route 41.

Because of their width, the RTWs were not initially permitted to operate in central London, nor along roads where trams were still running. This restricted their use to suburban routes, early allocations including Tottenham, Alperton, Shepherds Bush and Hanwell. In May 1950 London Transport conducted the first of three trials to show that these wider vehicles could work safely in the restricted areas of London. All services running through Notting Hill Gate were to be taken over by RTWs, brought in exchange for RT and RTL types. Similar trials were held in Shaftesbury Avenue and Threadneedle Street during the June and July. The results were successful and the redeployment of the RTWs took place in several stages between February and August 1951, during which time routes 6, 6A, 8, 8A, 11, 15, 22, 34B, 46, 76 and 100 were converted to RTW operation.

Garages receiving the new type included Willesden, Clayhall, Dalston, Riverside, Tottenham and Upton Park. The class continued in service in central London throughout the 1950s and into the 1960s, although the high point in the lives of RTW421 and 422 was their use on a promotional tour to Berlin in October 1950. Although strictly a non-standard class, the RTWs remained

Below:
RTW262 sits opposite Willesden garage in 1958, working on route 8 towards Oxford Circus. Behind is Leyland Routemaster RML3, then on trial, also on route 8. RTW262 was one of the 279 RTWs to find further work in Ceylon. *Kevin Lane Collection*

Opposite top:
Among the last routes to be operated by RTWs was the 109 from Brixton. RTW345 is seen on this duty towards the end of its life with London Transport. This was also one of the RTWs which ended up in Ceylon. *Kevin Lane Collection*

Opposite below:
Fewer than 20 RTWs saw further service with independent operators in this country, in contrast to the many RTLs. As a case in point, we have Barton's only RTW flanked by two of the company's more numerous RTLs inside Ilkeston garage in the late 1960s. RTW341 became Barton 1035, while 1033 and 1037 were formerly RTL1537 and RTL1483, all arriving in 1965. Three further RTLs were bought in 1965, with seven in 1966 and a final 11 in 1968. Furthermore, two Craven-bodied RTs were added with the acquisition of Cream Bus Services, Stamford, in 1961, thus all three postwar types were represented. RTW341 and RTL1483 were withdrawn in 1971, RTL1537 having been taken out of service in 1970. *Kevin Lane Collection*

in passenger service until May 1966, when the last ran from Brixton garage, while many went on to become driver trainers, in which capacity they survived until June 1970. Few others saw further service in this country: over half of the class was sold to the Ceylon Transport Board between 1965 and 1967. Eight RTWs have been preserved in this country, while one or two others may still survive abroad.

Class SRT

Chassis: AEC Regent (refurbished STL)
Bodywork: Park Royal (RT)
Numbers: SRT 1-160
Total: 160
Dates new: 1949/50

In common with many other operators in the immediate postwar period, London Transport embarked on a programme of fitting new bodies onto elderly but more-or-less sound chassis. The London case was slightly different in that it was intended as a temporary measure. Bodies for the RT class were being built at a faster rate than the chassis and so rather than slowing down their delivery, it was decided to fit these surplus bodies onto modernised STL chassis whose own Park Royal bodywork was deteriorating and in need of replacement.

The first 125 members of the SRT class were taken from the STL2516-2647 batch, dating from 1939. Amongst the modifications carried out were the reshaping and redrilling of the frames, the fitting of an RT radiator in a lower position and the use of RT steering gear. Thus with the fitting of new Park Royal bodies these vehicles looked for all the world like brand-new buses, although their old FJJ/FXT registrations rather gave the game away to those in the know.

This first batch of SRTs entered service between March and November 1949 with initial allocations to Palmers Green, Camberwell, Forest Gate, Gillingham Street and Chalk Farm for routes 34, 35, 96, 10 and 24 respectively. Their performance alongside the RTs left a lot to be desired, their inadequate brakes and underpowered engine together with heavier bodywork affecting their speed and hill climbing abilities. Because of this a good deal of reallocation took place to find more suitable areas of operation, including Cricklewood, Holloway and Barking.

The original intention was to build 300 of the class, but an improvement in RT delivery kept this down to 160, the last 35 being taken from the best of earlier STLs, with a mixture of DLU/DYL/DGX/EGO/ELP registrations. Withdrawal took place between July 1953 and August 1954, the biggest concentrations of the class ending up at Cricklewood and Chalk Farm garages. The bodies were all subsequently joined with RT chassis in the number series RT4397-4556, the last of which (by then on RT3800) survived until the end of the RTs in 1979. All of the STL chassis ended up as scrap.

Below:
Looking like a typical postwar RT, the prewar registration reveals that it is actually an SRT, in this case SRT2 constructed from the chassis of STL2520 and the Park Royal body later to appear on RT4440. It is working a Clapham Common-bound route 5 according to the blind, although it displays a 5A beneath the canopy, the location is Worcester Park station. The date is September 1949, SRT2 having entered service during the previous April. It lasted until December 1953. *A. B. Cross*

Class RLH

Chassis: AEC Regent III
Bodywork: Weymann
Numbers: RLH1-76
Total: 76
Dates new: 1950/52

Below:
RLH52 presents a fine sight in Redhill, working on route 447 from Merstham in the early 1960s. RLHs were introduced on this route from October 1954, the type being required because of the twin railway bridges in Battlebridge Lane, Merstham. *Alan Mortimer*

As was noted in the section dealing with the STLs, London Transport had but a small requirement for low-height buses. While new, vehicles would have been due during the early part of the 1950s, this was pre-empted by Midland General, now under BTC control who offered 20 Weymann-bodied AEC Regents, part of an order for 30 that they didn't now need. They looked very much the provincial bus with their high bonnet line and tall radiator and differed from the RT in many respects. These 20 buses became RLH1-20 and were registered KYY 501-20. They entered service during the summer of 1950 and were allocated to Amersham (1-6), Addlestone (7-14) and Godstone (15-20). This influx of new vehicles resulted in a major reshuffling of the existing lowbridge fleet of ST and STLs.

In order to standardise the lowbridge fleet, a further order was made for another 56 RLHs, 32 for the Country Area and the remaining 24 to be red for use in the Central Area. The chassis was the Regent 9613E model, similar to the first batch, but with a few London Transport modifications, the main difference being the polished aluminium radiators, as opposed to chrome used on the earlier vehicles. Identical Weymann bodies were fitted, and the buses were numbered RLH21-76 and registered MXX 221-76. All were delivered during late 1952 and early 1953. Notable on all RLHs was the one-piece destination screen at the front and nothing at all at the rear, although route number stencils were sometimes fitted to the lower back window. The Country Area allocation was shared amongst Godstone, Addlestone, Guildford, East Grinstead and Amersham, and included several routes not essential for lowbridge vehicles, but allowed the much needed luxury of spare buses. Of the Central Area buses, 14 went to Harrow Weald and 10 to Merton. This influx saw the swift demise of the remaining lowbridge ST, STL and the D classes.

The 1958 strike and subsequent cuts in service saw a reduction in RLH requirements. However, new route 178 operating from Dalston garage began in May 1959 using surplus vehicles, mainly from Merton. This route, as the 208A, had hitherto been single-deck worked and plagued by low bridges, some even too low for the RLHs, causing rerouteing and consequent renumbering.

The new decade saw a further decline in the use of the RLH. Perhaps the most well-known lowbridge route, the 410 (Bromley-Reigate), succumbed to RTs in 1964, although this was only possible by diverting to avoid the offending low bridge at Oxted station. By the time that the road had been lowered, RMLs were in charge.

By 1964 no new work could be found for the redundant members of the class, and the first disposals took place. The 336 and 461A routes were converted to RF and RT operation respectively during 1965, at the end of which year there were 27 Central and 16 Country RLHs scheduled for Monday to Friday operation. The decline continued, although 17 members of the class passed to London Country in January 1970, only to be withdrawn and replaced by SMs by the August — the first ex-London Transport class to be removed from the books by the new owner. The red RLHs bowed out at Dalston in April 1971 on route 178, RLH61 performing the honours.

The majority of the class ended up going for export, their low height proving to be popular abroad. Most went to the USA, either direct or following use in this country. UK operators included Samuel Ledgard of Leeds who took several early withdrawals (all of which later went to the United States), Blue Line Coaches of Upminster and Whippet of Hilton. RLH23/29/32 and 48 were preserved in Britain, although RLH29 later went to Switzerland, while RLH44 has been preserved in its final role with London Country, as a mobile uniform store. Curiously, RLH76 survives, almost submerged in other scrap, in a Staffordshire scrapyard where it has been since 1973.

Above:
The Cambridgeshire independent operator, Whippet Coaches of Hilton, ran RLH37/38/48, all acquired in May 1965 (joining RT546/677). Former RLH48, seen in the operator's yard in 1967, was the last to go, in 1974. Following a number of years in use as a promotional vehicle in Belgium, it was secured for preservation back in England. *Kevin Lane Collection*

Below:
Harrow Weald's RLH74 on local route 230 (Rayners Lane-Northwick Park station) on 11 June 1969. It is passing beneath the railway bridge in Headstone Lane, Wealdstone, which required the use of low-height vehicles. Three days later, the RLHs were replaced by flat-fare MBS route H1. *V. C. Jones/IAL*

Class RFW

Chassis: AEC Regal IV
Bodywork: Eastern Coach Works
Numbers: RFW1-15
Total: 15
Date new: 1951

With the majority of the private hire fleet of RFs coming into service, another variation on the AEC Regal IV joined them for similar duties. With their 30ft by 8ft 39-seat ECW bodywork, the RFW class of 15 vehicles was larger and more luxurious than its predecessors. The livery was the same as that carried by the RFs, but notably no destination screen was fitted, suggesting intended use on conducted tours. The choice of Eastern Coach Works as the bodybuilder was also noteworthy — the reason being that the Government wanted London Transport to use the newly nationalised company. (Apart from the GS class of 1953 and RMC4 in 1957, no bodywork came from this manufacturer until the BL/BS class Bristols in the mid-1970s.)

The class entered service during May and June 1951, initially from eight garages: Northfleet, Reigate, Windsor and Watford were allocated one each, while Romford took two and Putney, Dalston and Old Kent Road received three each. They replaced the LTC and TF classes, as did the private hire fleet of RFs, although the RFWs were to outlive the private hire RFs for a short time, the last — RFW1/6/11/14, at Romford, London Road — surviving until October 1964. No less than 10 of the class were exported to Ceylon where several were still reported in service in 1981, while RFW11 ended up as an immobile caravan in Ireland. RFW6 and 14 have been preserved.

Above:
RFW15, numerically the last of this small class, seen on a private hire working when nearly new. It was one of the 10 exported to Ceylon in 1964. It was not withdrawn until 1981 and used as a source of spares. *V. C. Jones/IAL*

Below:
RFW3 seen around 1963, towards the end of its life with London Transport, on a private hire working. In 1964 it was converted to a mobile showroom and was finally scrapped in 1970. *V. C. Jones/IAL*

Class RF

Chassis: AEC Regal IV
Bodywork: Metro-Cammell
Numbers: RF1-700
Total: 700
Dates new: 1951-53

Towards the end of the 1940s it was recognised that the existing single-deck fleet would need replacing with a totally new design, with the private hire fleet requiring urgent attention before the Festival of Britain in 1951. A vehicle with an underfloor engine was decided upon, leading to the building of a prototype chassis by AEC, the Regal IV, in 1949. It was powered by an AEC 9.6 litre engine, carried Park Royal 40-seat bodywork and was registered UMP 227; it entered service from St Albans garage on route 355 in May 1950. The results from this vehicle were satisfactory enough for London Transport to place an order for 700 chassis, although bodywork was to be supplied by Metro-Cammell. UMP 227 was subsequently demonstrated to Scottish Omnibuses before returning to AEC for use as a works bus and was eventually preserved.

The first of the new buses were destined for the private hire fleet, arriving between April and June 1951 in time for the Festival of Britain. These were RF1-25 (LUC 201-25) and carried Metro-Cammell 35-seat bus bodies with observation windows along the roof, making them ideal for sightseeing duties. The maximum permitted length for single-deckers was changed from 27ft 6in to 30ft while these first RFs were being built, so they remained at the shorter length. All others were built as 30-footers, but all 700 were 7ft 6in wide. They were delivered alongside the RFW class replacing LTC and TF classes, entering service from Central Area garages at Streatham, Merton, Holloway, Camberwell, Hammersmith, Upton Park and Middle Row. The class carried on with these private hire and sightseeing duties until 1956 when 10 vehicles were drawn from the batch as required for Green Line work. RF16-25 were outshopped in full Green Line colours and also received luggage racks and roof route boards. It was not unknown for these to make an occasional appearance on bus work, too.

The entire batch of 25 was withdrawn during 1962-63 and was put up for disposal. A number saw further PSV work, including eight with Premier Travel, Cambridge, while six are currently preserved.

The first of the 30ft RFs were for Green Line duties, numbered RF26-288 and registered LYF 377-476, MLL 513-612 and MLL 763-825. Metro-Cammell 39-seat bodies were fitted and were finished in Lincoln green with a lighter green around the windows. RF26-31 were in service at Tunbridge Wells in October

Below:
RF19 of the private hire batch, repainted into Green Line livery and seen at Golders Green in 1956. The roof-board shows it to be on route 716, Chertsey to Hitchin, a journey of nearly three hours. RF19 was withdrawn in 1962 and passed through a number of owners until purchased for preservation in 1980. *G. H. F. Atkins*

Right:
Several of the private hire RFs ended up in Ireland, including RF21, seen here with Kavanagh, Urlingford, in August 1964, a year after it was acquired, along with RF20, from Super Coaches of Upminster. *Mike Sutcliffe*

1951, with the last few arriving in October 1952, acting as spares. This swift entry into service of so many new vehicles saw the complete replacement of prewar stock on Green Line work, the ousted 10T10, TF and 6Q6 types often finding themselves on bus work in both the Central and Country Areas before final withdrawal. Thus, all Green Line services were in the capable hands of the RF, with the exception of the Romford-allocated RTs.

RF289-513 were buses for the Central Area and were registered MLL 926-995, MXX 1-30, MXX 277-299 and MXX 389-490. They were fitted with 41-seat Metro-Cammell bodies, although the Metropolitan Police still stipulated that no doors should be fitted as they were thought to delay boarding at stops. Livery was red with cream around the windows and black mudguards. The first into service, in September 1952, were RF289-91 at Muswell Hill for the 210 replacing TDs which in turn replaced 6Q6s on the 244. The type quickly spread around the system, replacing prewar classes as they went. By the time that the last had entered service, RF513 at Sidcup in March 1953, few prewar vehicles were left, the remaining former Green Line 10T10s at Enfield bowing out two months later. The Central Area single-deck fleet was now composed of just RF, TD and 14T12 types.

The final RFs were buses for the Country Area: RF514-700, registered NLE 514-700. Their 41-seat Metro-Cammell bodies were similar to those for the Central Area, although doors were fitted. Livery was Lincoln green with cream window surrounds and green mudguards. The first examples were in service by March 1953, RF514-6 at Reigate, heralding the end of the 4Q4s, while all but three were at work by the December. These exceptions were RF517/647/700, converted to OMO for its evaluation which was conducted at Leatherhead and later Hemel Hempstead.

By the middle of the 1950s it was evident that the existing Green Line fleet of RFs would not be sufficient to cope with the demands of the increasing network. As noted above, 10 of the private hire RFs were converted for Green Line use in 1955-56. So far so good. However, it was later decided to draw on members of the bus fleet for conversion and at the same time effect a renumbering scheme so as to keep the various vehicle types together. In total 25 vehicles were involved, six from the Central Area, the rest from the Country Area. Red RFs 289-94 were fitted with doors and repainted, retaining their numbers. Those from the Country fleet needed little more than a repaint. These were RF514-6, becoming RF295-7; RF518-32, becoming RF299-313; and RF697, which became RF298. The original RF295-313 thus became RF514-32.

From June 1959 a number of Country RTs were used as Green Line duplicate and spare vehicles, thus releasing RFs onto Country routes where crewed vehicles could be justified. The first major change to the Green Line RFs came in 1962 with the introduction of Routemaster coaches — the RMCs. The first casualties were the former private hire vehicles, RF16-25, which were withdrawn and the 1956 conversions, RF298-313, which became buses again, mostly at Amersham to replace GSs. From 1963, Green Line operations declined and the fleet was further depleted when a number of surplus coaches were sold in 1964-65.

In 1966 a pilot refurbishment was carried out on RF136; treatment included fluorescent lighting, twin headlamps, a new one-piece driver's windscreen and a revised livery featuring a wide green band. This modernisation was deemed to be a success and by July 1967 174 further vehicles had been completed. Early in 1967 conversion to OMO was included in the facelift, all but 25 being so fitted. These became buses and were eventually fitted for OMO. There was a surplus of coaches at this time occasioned by a general decline in usage. There were many factors involved in this, not least the severe traffic congestion causing problems with timekeeping. The remaining Green Line coaches, all except the 1964-65 withdrawals, passed to the newly formed London Country Bus Services in 1970. Withdrawals commenced in 1971, with only RF202 surviving until the company was split in 1986. A number of the former Green Line batch have been preserved.

As we have seen, six of the Central Area red RFs were converted to Green Line coaches in 1956. These were replaced by six green RFs at Sidcup, joining others which had already been allocated there because of shortages. These six, RF533-38, were later painted red and had their doors removed. Around a year later, in April 1959, these six buses were part of a batch (RF502-38) experimentally converted to OMO and with their doors restored! Trade Union opposition to this method of operation saw these buses used as crewed buses (with their doors bolted open) or as one-man buses in the Country Area. OMO did not start in the Central Area until November 1964, with the last crewed RF finally running in 1971.

The early 1970s saw the red RFs withdrawn in some numbers, often to be replaced by AEC Swifts; 1976 was a particularly bad year, following the introduction of the BL class. The last RFs eventually ran from Kingston in March 1979, a batch of 25 recertified vehicles used on routes 218/9. Many of the type passed to non-PSV use and their longevity has ensured a healthy number in preservation.

The Country Area RFs were subject to conversion to OMO long before their red counterparts, with economies essential to the survival of many of the more rural routes. The 1954 trials were quite successful, leading to wholesale OMO, the last RFs with conductors running at St Albans and Reigate in 1959 (although crew-operated Green Line RFs did continue for a while on routes 355 and 447). Most of the Country Area RFs passed to London Country in 1969, with the exception of a small number transferred previously to the Central Area. Withdrawals took place throughout the 1970s until the last one, RF684 at Chelsham, was taken out of service in May 1978. As with the red RFs, most subsequent disposals were of a non-PSV nature, with a number subsequently preserved.

Above:
A December 1967 view of Green Line RF228 after its modernisation, standing on the square in Dunstable waiting to leave for Dorking, a journey of just over three hours — traffic permitting. This facility has long since ceased to exist; the easiest way to get to Dorking from Dunstable today would be to go to Luton by bus and then get a train. RF228 was withdrawn by London Country at Dorking in 1972 and stripped for spares. *Chris Lodington*

Opposite top:
RF471 leads RF520 (formerly RF301), both Kingston-bound in Esher during March 1979, the last month of RF operation. Both ended up as scrap with Booth, Rotherham by the end of the year. *Kevin Lane*

Opposite below:
Country Area RF569 waiting to return to Hertford bus station from Buntingford in 1965. RF569 duly passed to London Country in 1970, being withdrawn in February 1973 from Crawley, passing locally into non-PSV use and later being converted into a car transporter. *V. C. Jones/IAL*

218
KINGSTON
219
KINGSTON
PAY AS YOU ENTER
MXX 448
NLL 938

HERTFORD
LONDON TRANSPORT
RF 569
NLE569

Class GS

Chassis: Guy 'Special' **Total:** 84
Bodywork: Eastern Coach Works **Date new:** 1953
Numbers: GS1-84

Towards the end of 1953, with the delivery of the 700-strong RF class nearing completion, London Transport introduced a rather smaller, more specialised type — the little GS. Based on a modified Guy Vixen chassis, but with certain features specified by London Transport (hence GS, Guy Special), the buses were normal-control, powered by Perkins P6 six-cylinder oil engines. Bodywork was by Eastern Coach Works, seating 26, and the result was a most attractive looking vehicle.

The GS was built for those routes where even the RF was too large, and replaced, in the main, the prewar C and CR class Leyland Cubs. Numbered GS1-84, they were registered MXX 301-384. The class entered service throughout the Country Area during 1953-54 (except for GS84, which was stored until 1956). An interesting interlude early in their lives was the loan of five vehicles, GS61, 63, 68, 70 and 72, to Great Yarmouth Corporation to get OMO started in the town in 1958-59. Also, many of the class were used as training or staff buses during the 1960s.

The general decline in rural services saw the first withdrawal as early as 1957, GS32/43 being the first to go. Thereafter, a steady reduction in numbers continued throughout the 1960s as work for them disappeared. Eighteen of the class survived to be transferred to London Country in 1970, although eight of these were in a withdrawn state. The last in service were GS33/42, withdrawn from Garston, where they were used on the 336A, at the end of March 1972.

The GS was a useful little bus which travelled far and wide after its disposal by London Transport. Independents to operate them included Tillingbourne Valley, Chilworth, Southern Motorways, Emsworth, Corvedale Motor Services of Ludlow and Bickers of Coddenham. Other buyers included British Railways and, notably, West Bromwich Corporation; many others saw non-PSV use. Around 27, almost a third of the class, have been preserved, with possibly several others still extant — two had apparently survived with travellers into the 1990s.

Below:
GS by the sea! GS61 on hire to Great Yarmouth Corporation, seen outside Vauxhall railway station in 1958. GS61 was one of five to pass to Corvedale Motor Co, Ludlow, in 1961. Withdrawn in May 1965, having swapped registrations with GS63 to become MXX 363, it served with a number of operators to end up in non-PSV use in Norfolk in 1969. *Ron Wellings*

Opposite top:
Amersham garage forecourt in 1962, with GS56 and GS28 awaiting further duties. GS56 has apparently worked a garage journey in from route 348, Buckland Common-Chesham Moor. GS56 was withdrawn from Dunton Green in December 1966, later passing to Bickers of Coddenham together with GS60. Both were preserved in 1976. GS28 survived with London Transport until June 1968 at Northfleet and subsequently became transport for a rock band and later a caravan, being re-registered BSV 910. *Alan Mortimer*

Opposite bottom:
GS6 was acquired by the Top Rank Organisation in 1963 and was based at Farthing Corner services on the M2. In 1967 it served with St John's College, Horsham, until sold as a caravan in 1974. *V. C. Jones/IAL*

AMERS
LONDON TRANSPORT
AMERSHAM
348 VIA
GS 56
LONDON TRANSPORT
MXX 356
PRIVATE
MXX 328
NO ENTRY
FOR THE PUBLIC

VISIT THE
RESTAURANTS
ON THE M.2 AT
FARTHING CORNER
Top Rank MOTORWAY SERVICE
MXX 306

Class RM/RML/RMC/RCL/RMA/ RMF/RMT/ERM

Chassis: AEC Routemaster
Bodywork: Eastern Coach Works/Park Royal/Weymann
Numbers: RM/RML/RMC/RCL/ERM — 1-2760, RMA1-65, RMF1254/2761-72, RMT2793
Totals: RM/RML/RMC/RCL/ERM — 2,760
RMA — 65
RMF — 13
RMT — 1
Dates new: 1954-68

It must be something of a record that the Routemaster, still a common sight on the streets of London, first saw the light of day over 40 years ago, such has been its success. The development of a replacement for the trolleybuses began before the delivery of the last RT, RM1 being built at Park Royal in 1954.

New thought was given to this new generation of London bus; improved body design and the use of two subframes rather than a complete chassis gave a bus the same laden weight as an RT but with seating for 64 rather than 56. RM1 was the prototype Central Area bus. Its aluminium alloy body was built by London Transport and Park Royal and an AEC AV590 9.6 litre engine was fitted. As built, there was no room for the radiator in the conventional position within the maximum 27ft by 8ft dimensions; it was positioned under the cab. A smooth front panel with a bullseye replaced the more usual radiator grille, although when longer double-deckers were allowed the radiator was put back at the front, with the familiar grille in place. RM1 was registered SLT 56 (the originally intended OLD 862 no doubt being deemed unsuitable) and eventually went to work on route 2 (Golders Green-Crystal Palace) in February 1956 from Cricklewood garage.

RM2, registered SLT 57, had a number of detail differences, including the fitting of a smaller 7.7 litre AEC engine, and went to Reigate for Country Area service in May 1957, over two years after completion. It found little favour there and had been transferred to the Central Area at Turnham Green by the September, being fitted with a more powerful 9.6 litre engine.

RML3, registered SLT 58, was bodied by Weymann and was powered by a Leyland 0600 9.8 litre engine and featured a side-opening bonnet. This 27ft 6in bus entered service at Willesden garage on route 8 (Kingsbury-Old Ford) in January 1958. It was renumbered RM3 in 1961.

The last of the prototypes was Green Line coach CRL4, registered SLT 59. Leyland running units were fitted and the 57-seat body was built by Eastern Coach Works, the vehicle entering service from Romford London Road garage in October 1957. It was renumbered RMC4 in 1961.

Production of the Routemaster got under way with the first bus entering service in June 1959. AEC was the preferred choice of

Below:
RM1 entered service in February 1956 on route 2 from Cricklewood garage, switching onto route 260 in March 1957 following modifications, including the fitting of a more conventional looking radiator grille. It is seen here shortly after entering service and, like RM2 and RML3, was transferred to training duties from November 1959. *John Hambley Collection*

Right:
Of the four prototypes, CRL4, the Green Line coach, lasted the longest in passenger service, passing to London Country in 1970 (by then renumbered RMC4) and being withdrawn in May 1979. In this fine view around 1962, CRL4 pulls out into traffic at Golders Green on route 716A, Stevenage-Woking via Barnet and Kingston. The journey would have then taken 3hr 14min at a single fare of 10s 3d, a little over 50p! *Alan Mortimer*

engine, while the bodies were by Park Royal. First to arrive was RM8, displaying a modified, and subsequently standard, front end. Initially, the first buses went into normal service, although by the end of 1959 they were released only for trolleybus replacement until this was completed in 1962. From then on, RT, RTL and RTW replacement was the priority.

In 1961 came the first 30ft long Routemasters, ER880-903, although they were reclassified RML before delivery; they were 72-seaters easily recognisable by the extra half-window incorporated into the body. Route 104 (Barnet-Moorgate), operated from Finchley garage, was their first stamping ground. Routemasters were also acquired from Northern General between 1978 and 1980; two were stripped for spares, but plans to overhaul the others for passenger service sadly fell through. They were allotted fleet numbers, RMF2761-72. Some were later hired back to LT for sightseeing duties by the dealer, Brakell.

Another significant acquisition was that of the British Airways Routemasters. As recounted elsewhere, 65 front-entrance Routemasters were operated by LT between the Gloucester Road air terminal and Heathrow. As the need for them diminished they were gradually bought by LT from 1975. The first batch was used in service on route 175 at Romford for a period, but the vehicles were later used for driver training, while many of the later acquisitions became staff buses and could be seen well out of London. They were numbered RMA1-65.

The first production Routemasters for Green Line duties were RMC1453-1520, which began to replace RFs from August 1962. Their Park Royal bodies seated 57 and were similar to that on RMC4 but also included fluorescent lighting. Further coaches were 30ft long — RCL2218-60, new in 1965, to initially replace RTs on the 721/722/723 group of services. RM construction continued until 1965, last in the line being RM2217 (CUV 217C). Following the delivery of the RCLs, production was concentrated on RMLs, including 100 with semi-automatic gearboxes for the Country Area, RML2306-55 and 2411-60. Upton Park's RML2760 was the very last, going into service in March 1968. Few operators other than LT supported the Routemaster, only Northern General and British Airways taking any interest. A front-entrance Routemaster, numbered RMF1254 and registered 254 CLT, was built in 1962 as a demonstrator. Due to union opposition it did not run for London Transport, but was loaned to British European Airways in 1964-66 before being sold to Northern General.

The first big upheaval in the fleet occurred with the transfer on 1 January 1970 to the newly formed London Country Bus Services of the Country Area vehicles: 97 RMLs, 69 RMCs and 43 RCLs, the odd three RMLs having been exchanged with three XAs in 1969. Many of these subsequently returned to the fold and have seen use as training buses and in service. Fourteen

The Central Area Routemasters, with a few exceptions, survived intact until 1982, although the 1966 Reshaping Plan could have seen their elimination nearly 10 years before. Some interesting liveries have adorned the class during this period. The Queen's Silver Jubilee saw 25 RMs given overhauls, painted silver and fitted with carpets. They were renumbered SRM1-25, working on various routes between April and November 1977 before repainting. Between March and November 1979 12 RMs received the dark green and yellow George Shillibeer livery commemorating 150 years of bus operation in London, while between April and September of the same year, a further 16 RMs worked a special 'Shoplinker' service in the West End wearing a startling red and yellow livery. The wedding of HRH The Prince of Wales to Lady Diana Spencer prompted eight RMs to be painted up like wedding gifts; these were used between June and November 1981.

The first Routemaster withdrawals in quantity occurred in 1982 following the decision of the Law Lords that the Fares Fair policy of the Greater London Council was unlawful. Up went the fares again, and down, inevitably, went the numbers of people using the buses. Over 200 Routemasters were declared surplus, many of

Above:
Production of the Routemaster got under way in 1958, although the first did not enter service until June 1959. RM1089 was put on the road in May 1962 so would have been brand-new in this picture. The location is Kingston Road, Malden, and RM1089 is passing beneath recently abandoned trolleywires on route 285, itself introduced on 9 May, the day following the end of trolleybus operation in London. *Kevin Lane Collection*

Below:
To celebrate the Queen's Silver Jubilee in 1977, 25 RMs gained a silver livery and were renumbered SRM1-25, working on routes through central London. RM1920 became SRM16 and is pictured in Battersea Rise on route 19, today operated by Kentish Bus RMLs, although they no longer reach this far. *Kevin Lane Collection*

Above:
The pre-production RMLs (880-903) were all allocated to Finchley garage in 1961 for route 104 (Moorgate-Barnet), which replaced trolleybus route 609. Here RML880 is seen at Moorgate in 1964. In all 23 of these RMLs passed to nine of the privatised companies; the one that escaped was RML900, which was sold as accident-damaged to Clydeside Scottish in 1988 and rebuilt using parts from RM1984. *V. C. Jones/IAL*

Below:
Like the RTs before them, a number of Routemasters have taken part in overseas goodwill trips over the years. In April and May 1968 RMLs 2548 and 2560 sailed to Esbjerg, Denmark, to take part in a British Week there. RML2548 is seen aboard the United Steamship Co Ltd of Copenhagen (DFDS) ferry, MS *Stafford*, at Harwich on 18 April. In the previous December these two RMLs had returned from a trip to Expo '67 in Canada, while RML2548 was to make a final overseas trip in September 1968 to Switzerland. In between these last two visits, RML2548 had briefly entered service at Chalk Farm garage, returning there in the October. *DFDS*

these subsequently going for scrap. However, as described below, deregulation brought an unexpected change of fortune for the Routemaster in the provinces.

Although the fleet of Routemasters was gradually on the decrease, some interesting developments were taking place. A programme of re-engining over 400 Routemasters with either Cummins or Iveco power units commenced in 1990, while from 1992 nearly 500 RMLs were refurbished to see them into the 21st century. Features include double-dip headlamps, fluorescent interior and blind-box lighting, new heating systems and the fitting of DiPTAC features. Mechanical parts were also replaced as necessary, to aid economy and maintenance. 1986 had seen the transfer of 50 Routemasters to what was to become London Coaches. These were used on a variety of sightseeing and private hire operations and were variously converted for these roles. This has included the conversion of many to open-top, while more drastic surgery has involved the fitting of an extra bay into 10 open-top RMs, thus making them 72-seaters. These were reclassified ERM (Extended Routemaster), retaining their original numbers. When London Coaches was privatised in May 1992 it took 11 RCLs, the 10 ERMs and 18 RMs.

When it was discovered that the Routemaster was a useful weapon in the deregulation war, offering speedy loading and unloading and an undoubted novelty value, operators using the type sprang up all over the country, prompting London bus enthusiasts to travel to many unlikely places. Bedford, Blackpool, Burnley, Reading, Bournemouth, Southampton, Hull, Glasgow, Southend — the list went on and on. Furthermore, the tendering process brought independent Routemaster operation into London. Kentish Bus uses leased RMLs on the 19 (Finsbury Park-Battersea Bridge) and BTS, now Sovereign, has them for the 13 (Golders Green-Aldwych). A number of Routemasters have gone abroad, while the non-PSV uses of the type are many and various. Many have been preserved, including RM1-3 and RMC4, and no doubt many more will follow. All of the privatised companies took over Routemasters with the exception of Westlink, the two RMCs with Selkent being for special duties. The lowest numbered buses to survive with the new companies were RM5 with Leaside Buses, RM6 with South London and RM9 with London Central.

Above:
1962 saw the arrival of Routemaster coaches RMC1453-1520 for Green Line duties. RMC1479 stands in the sunshine outside its home garage, Windsor, in 1964, having worked in on the long journey from Harlow. The entire batch passed to London Country in 1970, with many returning to London Transport at the end of the 1970s. RMC1479 became a training bus with London Transport, still in green livery, but was one of a batch of RMCs declared surplus in 1981 and sold for scrap after stripping at Aldenham. *V. C. Jones/IAL*

Below:
The lengthened Routemaster coaches, the RCLs, also passed back to London Transport at the same time as the RMCs, and although they too were initially used as training buses, they were destined for greater things. In 1980 the 40 survivors (2221 became an exhibition bus and 2225/7 were sold for scrap) were put back into passenger service, following modification, on routes 149 and 279. Here RCL2238 waits at Waltham Cross on route 279 (Hammond Street-Smithfield) in November 1983. The RCLs were replaced by surplus RMs at the end of 1984, RCL2238 passing into non-PSV use as a catering vehicle with a film company. *Kevin Lane*

Above:
London Transport took all 65 front-entrance Routemasters from British Airways in 1975/6/9; in the main they saw use as staff or training buses. RMA24, still in its former BA blue and white livery, is seen in Luton on staff duties from Aldenham in August 1979. *Kevin Lane*

Below:
Deregulation saw the Routemaster turning up all over the place in the battle for customers. Southampton Citybus put RMs onto several routes during 1987 in order to compete with Solent Blue-Line which was using crew-operated Bristol VRTs. Here 402 (RM1793) and 408 (RM1713) pass in the city in October 1987, the latter being followed by a Solent Blue-Line VRT, also going to Shirley and Millbrook. Routemaster operation ceased in January 1989, although a couple were retained, appearing over Christmas 1990. RM1713 has been scrapped and RM1793 was later exported to Japan. *Kevin Lane*

Class RW

Chassis: AEC Reliance
Bodywork: Willowbrook
Numbers: RW1-3
Total: 3
Date new: 1960

These three vehicles were purchased to evaluate OMO and a dual-door layout in the Country Area. The AEC Reliance chassis were fitted with 42-seat Willowbrook dual-door bodies, of a type to be seen in the provinces — Grimsby-Cleethorpes, for example. Registered 495-497 ALH and numbered RW1-3, they entered service at Hemel Hempstead in September 1960. The trials took them to other Country Area garages, including Addlestone, Hertford and Reigate, although they ended up at St Albans where they were withdrawn in October 1963, unpopular with both drivers and engineers.

All three were soon sold to Chesterfield Corporation, becoming 18-20 in that fleet, joining other Reliances; they worked there until 1977-8. RW1 was sold for scrap, while RW2 went straight into preservation. RW3 served with a couple of West Country independents until it was also bought for preservation in 1988.

Above:
RW1 — the one that got away — pictured working a Watford Junction-bound 322 at Hemel Hempstead in August 1963. *Tony Wild*

Below:
RW3 during its days with Chesterfield Corporation, seen on 20 July 1973. *G. R. Mills*

Class TT

Chassis: Ford Thames Trader
Bodywork: Strachan
Numbers: TT1-5
Total: 5
Date new: 1963

In order to transport cyclists and their machines through the Dartford Tunnel, to whom it was barred between the hours of 06.00 and 20.00, the Dartford Tunnel Joint Committee bought five Strachan-bodied Ford Thames Traders, numbered TT1-5 and registered 526-30 FJJ, a rather optimistic gesture towards the cyclists as it turned out. A total of 23 cycles could be stored in the lower deck, while upstairs there was seating for 33, presumably to take into account the possibility of carrying a few tandems. Loading platforms were provided at Dartford and Purfleet, with access possible from both sides. The buses were operated on behalf of the Committee by LT and allocated at Dartford garage.

The service, requiring four vehicles, commenced in November 1963 but never came up to expectations. Before long, only one vehicle was required, this too being withdrawn and replaced by a Land Rover in September 1965. All passed to a Wolverhampton dealer in March 1966, TT1 later seeing experimental use in Scotland, while TT4 was sold to Shrewsbury Corporation, its purpose unknown.

Below:
TT2, with TT1 behind, at the Dartford side of the tunnel, on 23 November 1963, two months after the start of the service.
Tony Wild

Class DMO

Chassis: Daimler Fleetline CRG6LX
Bodywork: Weymann
Numbers: DMO1-7
Total: 7
Date new: 1965
Date acquired: 1977

These seven Daimler Fleetlines were acquired from Bournemouth in 1977 for sightseeing duties from the following year. They were Gardner-engined and carried Weymann bodies that were convertible to open-top form as required. They were registered CRU 182-87/89C and formed the DMO class. Dating from 1965, they were contemporaries of the XF class of Fleetlines. While in service with Bournemouth, they bore the names of English counties. Although these were lost on repainting in London, Stockwell garage later named the first three: DMO1-3 becoming *Stockwell Princess*, *Southern Queen* and *Britannia* respectively.

They were used on the Round London Sightseeing Tour until 1981 after which all except DMO3 were withdrawn, this vehicle surviving to take part in the London Transport Golden Jubilee celebrations in 1983. DMO1/7 were exported to Sweden, while DMO2/5 went to the United States and of the rest, DMO3 is still active with Guide Friday at Stratford-upon-Avon.

Below:
DMO1 on sightseeing duties at Victoria in 1979. Following withdrawal it was exported to Sweden along with DMO7.
Kevin Lane Collection

Class RC

Chassis: AEC Reliance
Bodywork: Willowbrook
Numbers: RC1-14
Total: 14
Date new: 1965

In a bid to improve the standard of Green Line travel, which in the mid-1960s involved using vehicles that were nearer buses than coaches in terms of comfort, a small class of 14 AEC Reliance 4U2RA chassis with 36ft Willowbrook dual-purpose 49-seat bodies were put into service from November 1965.

Numbered RC1-14 and registered CUV 59-72C, they featured a five-speed semi-automatic gearbox and air suspension and were finished in a grey livery with a broad green band, although this was later changed to the standard two-tone green. Roof-boards were fitted, although these were black on yellow rather than yellow on black.

They initially entered service from Dunton Green and Windsor garages on route 705, although their reliability was not good. Some were fitted with extra luggage racks and down-seated to 43 for use on route 727 during the spring of 1969. All of the class were transferred to London Country Bus Services on 1 January 1970 and most were delicensed only to appear on the 727 and later 723 routes, being demoted to bus work at Hertford by 1974. Most of the class survived in service until 1977, the last acting as driver trainers until 1979. All were sold for scrap without operating elsewhere.

Left:
RC14 in the familiar setting of Eccleston Bridge, Victoria, in May 1967, demonstrating the striking new livery style. It is working on Green Line route 705 from Sevenoaks to Windsor, a journey of 2hr 40min, traffic permitting! RC14 ended up relegated to bus work at Hertford with London Country and was sold for scrap in 1977. *G. H. F. Atkins*

Below:
Complete with the 'flying polo' on the front panel, RC11 in early London Country days at Aldgate after arrival on a 723 journey from Grays. RC11 was the first of the class to be withdrawn, gutted by fire in August 1971. *V. C. Jones/IAL*

Class XA

Chassis: Leyland Atlantean PDR1/1
Bodywork: Park Royal
Numbers: XA1-50
Total: 50
Date new: 1965

The year 1965 saw the delivery of the 50 evaluatory Leyland Atlanteans, to be pitched against the Daimler Fleetline and the RML. Park Royal 72-seat bodies to standard provincial design were fitted; these were notable in having sliding ventilators, rather than the traditional (for London) wind-down windows.

Numbered XA1-50 and registered CUV 1-37C and JLA 38-50D they arrived during the second half of the year, the first going into service on route 24 (Hampstead Heath to Pimlico) in the November, a couple of months after the XF class of Daimler Fleetline. The second route to receive the XAs was the 271 (Highgate Village to Moorgate) operated from Highgate garage, which commenced on the first day of 1966. These initial trials were against the RMLs which were now operating on routes 67 and 76.

Fuel consumption tests were carried out from April 1966, seeing the eight XFs at East Grinstead being swapped for the same number of XAs, the Atlanteans working on route 424 from Reigate to East Grinstead. Further changes in the June involved the XAs moving onto the 76, on which FRM1 was also running, with the RMLs taking their place on the 24. Highgate's XAs joined those returned from East Grinstead at Stamford Hill for service on the 67, the RMLs being moved on to the 271. While the test results saw the XA giving the best return in the Central Area (the RML came out on top in the Country Area), increased boarding times caused by the doors, even on crewed buses, was less acceptable than an open-platform RML.

The XAs saw service elsewhere, during their short lives with London Transport. In November 1969, XA22 became the first one-man-operated double-decker in London when it began service on route 233 at West Croydon, while farebox-fitted XAs worked on Peckham local route P3 from January 1970. Also at this time, XA46-8 had been inherited by the newly formed NBC subsidiary, London Country Bus Services, having gone to East Grinstead to release XFs for Blue Arrow duties in Stevenage during the previous month. A new network of express routes in Croydon saw the bulk of the class employed here from 1970.

The Atlanteans, being non-standard in the fleet as London Transport had decided on the Daimler Fleetline as the future double-deck bus, were vulnerable to early withdrawal. This came in 1973 when all 50, including the three with London Country, were sold to China Motor Bus, who, along with Kowloon Motor Bus, required large numbers of buses to work services through the new cross-harbour tunnel. They were replaced in London by DMSs, with the P3 going over to SMS operation.

Below:
XA2 leaving Waterloo for Tottenham garage and home on a 76 service in May 1969. *V. C. Jones/IAL*

Class XF

Chassis: Daimler Fleetline CRG6LX **Total:** 8
Bodywork: Park Royal **Date new:** 1965
Numbers: XF1-8

Eight Daimler Fleetlines with Park Royal H31/41F bodies entered service in September 1965 for evaluation in the Country Area. They were delivered alongside the XA class Leyland Atlanteans for the Central Area, offering comparison between the two types. The buses, numbered XF1-8 and registered CUV 51-58C, went to East Grinstead garage to replace RTs on the 424 (East Grinstead-Reigate). It had been intended to operate them as one-man buses, but as the required legislation was not forthcoming they ran as crewed vehicles.

Between April and July 1966 there was an exchange of vehicles for fuel consumption tests. Thus the eight Fleetlines at East Grinstead were swapped with eight Atlanteans from Holloway garage. The XFs were used on the 271 route (Highgate Village-Moorgate) alongside other XAs.

From October 1966, following a change in the regulations, the XFs, now back on the 424, were able to operate as one-man buses provided that the top deck was sealed off. This was not particularly satisfactory as it gave seating for only 31 at such times — less than the capacity of an RF. Furthermore, a conductor had to be employed if the top deck was in use. Full crew operation was resumed in April 1967 and shortly afterwards the XFs went on their travels again, this time to Stamford Hill for trials on the 67 (Northumberland Park-Wapping), again in exchange for XAs. Also in 1967, XF3 was fitted with a Cummins V6 engine in lieu of its Gardner 6LX; this experiment lasted until 1973.

Almost at the end of their time with London Transport, three of the class, XF6-8, were repainted blue and silver for a new works service in Stevenage. Named 'Blue Arrow', the service was dedicated for workers travelling from Chells to the industrial areas of the new town, commencing just three days before the Country Area was transferred to London Country. All eight XFs passed to London Country, and were all back at East Grinstead by 1972. The class lasted until 1981, with XF3 achieving the distinction of being the last former London Transport vehicle to remain in normal service with London Country. XF3 was subsequently preserved, along with XF1.

Below:
XF1 and XF8 stand at Moorgate on route 271 in May 1966, during the period that they were working in the Central Area from Holloway garage. *A. G. Low*

Bottom:
XF5 in more usual surroundings on an East Grinstead-bound route 424 journey in 1965 when new. *V. C. Jones/IAL*

Class FRM

Chassis: AEC Routemaster FR2R **Total:** 1
Bodywork: Park Royal **Date new:** 1966
Number: FRM1

The rear-engined Routemaster was very much a 'what might have been'. Designed by London Transport, AEC and Park Royal, work started in 1964. At this time, one-man operation of double-deckers was not permitted in London, although it was seen to be only a matter of time before it would be. The first of what had been intended to be a small number of prototypes appeared in 1966 and became FRM1 (Front-entrance Routemaster) and was registered KGY 4D. It became the first integral double-decker with a rear engine to be built in this country and was built using around 60 per cent of Routemaster parts. The power was provided by an AEC AV691 engine situated transversely at the rear, while the Park Royal body seated 72. Full air-conditioning was fitted and so no opening windows were fitted, although early experience saw the reversal of this decision.

Following the usual testing, FRM1 entered service from Tottenham garage on route 76 (Victoria-Tottenham) alongside XA class Leyland Atlanteans in June 1967. It stayed with some success until sent to Chiswick for conversion to OMO, now legal, in August 1969. It reappeared at Croydon in the December, on London's first one-man double-deck service, route 233 (West Croydon station-Roundshaw Estate). It remained on the 233 until it was converted to SMS operation in March 1971, when it was transferred to the 234/234B (Selsdon-Hackbridge/South Croydon), again alongside XAs. With the withdrawal of the XA class, FRM1 was put into store in January 1973 as it was not possible to use the bus alongside the dual-door replacement DMSs.

Despite now being the only one of its kind, FRM1 was given an overhaul and returned to service at Potters Bar in October 1973, seeing service on local route 284, on which it was the only vehicle. Here it stayed for nearly three years until an accident put it out of service in September 1976. By the time that repairs had been effected, route 284 had been withdrawn, so FRM1 was put onto the Round London Sightseeing Tour, operating from first Stockwell and latterly Victoria. It remained on this duty for some seven years (how many of its passengers realised the significance of their bus, I wonder?) until it was donated to the London Transport Museum in 1984.

Above right:
An offside rear view of FRM1, taken during its first weeks in service. The bus caught fire on 31 August and the non-opening windows had to be smashed by the Fire Brigade to allow the smoke inside to escape. It was subsequently fitted with standard Routemaster quarter-drop winding windows, re-entering service in December 1967. *Kevin Lane Collection*

Below:
The FRM worked the 233 from December 1969 until March 1971, when it was replaced by an SMS. It is seen in 1970 at Roundshaw, waiting to return to West Croydon. *Michael Fowler*

Class XMB/XMS/MB/MBA/MBS

Chassis: AEC Swift 4P4R
Total: 665
Bodywork: Strachan/Metro-Cammell
Dates new: 1966-69
Numbers: XMB/XMS/MB/MBA/ MBS 1-665

When London Transport turned to large capacity single-deckers in the mid-1960s, it naturally turned to AEC and the rear-engined Swift model, built at Southall since 1964. In order to evaluate the type, 15 were bought for both Central and Country operation. The six for the Central Area were classified XMS, numbered 1-6 and registered JLA 51-56D. They were fitted with 36ft Strachan B25D+48 bodywork and they entered service on the pioneer Red Arrow route 500 in April 1966. The Country Area batch were XMB1-9, registered JLA 57-65D, with bodywork again by Strachan, this time as 46-seaters with no standing area. These did not enter service due to disputes over OMO. The power unit was the 11.3 litre AEC AH691. However, such was the success of the Red Arrow service, that XMB2-9 were also converted for this use and became XMS7-14. XMB1, which received the registration SMM 15F (JLA 57D not being used) and renumbered XMB15 in 1966, was trialled during 1967-68 at Reigate and Garston.

A further 150 Merlins, as the class was dubbed, were subsequently ordered, numbered in the same series. These were all bodied by Metro-Cammell to a slightly less boxy design than those supplied by Strachan and with a different windscreen arrangement. As originally designated, these 150 were classified as follows: Red Arrow buses were MBA16-31, while MBS32-80 were for suburban flat-fare routes, both seating B25D+48 standing. MB81-113 were one-man buses for the Country Area, dual-doored and seating 45, while MB114-65 were Central Area one-man buses seating 50. These should have entered service during the first part of 1968, but delays saw a number registered later in the year, hence the mixture of SMM-F and VLW-G marks.

Although little operating experience had been gained with the Merlins, a massive order for another 500 was made, with deliveries beginning early in 1968. These were split as follows: Red Arrow MBA166-93; suburban flat-fare MBS194-269 and MBS439-615; Country Area one-man (with standing area) MBS270-303 and MBS398-438; Central Area one-man MB304-97 and MB616-65. Metro-Cammell bodywork was used throughout and all vehicles featured a higher driving position, following complaints from the drivers. The last vehicle had been delivered by October 1969, by which time it was realised that the Merlins were just too long at 36ft for the conditions under which they were operating, resulting in manoeuvrability problems. The original idea was that a bus of such a length would be able to replace a double-decker, the RTs being 56-seaters. Subsequent AEC Swifts were of the shorter SM class.

The introduction of such a large number of buses enabled the withdrawal of elderly vehicles (such as RTs) and the implementation of OMO on a large scale — a high priority due to the prevailing severe staff shortages. The initial classifications were soon to change, early decisions included the original Red Arrow vehicles being rebuilt as MBs, with some MBSs taking their place. In 1970, 109 vehicles were transferred to London

Below:
Seen here on Red Arrow route 500 at Victoria in November 1967, XMS14 was formerly Country Area XMB9. In April 1970 it become MB14 when it was reseated to accommodate 45 passengers; it was withdrawn in May 1972. *G. R. Mills*

Country Bus Services on its formation, consisting of XMB15, MB81-113 and MBS270-303/398-438. An early casualty was Garston's MB101, destroyed by fire in the September while working on route 318A.

In 1972, MBS4 was given a pilot overhaul at Aldenham, with the resulting decision not to proceed with the others on cost grounds. Thus it was decided to dispose of the class, the prototypes going first and a start being made on the others from 1973-4, with those with the lower driving position going early on. Between 1974-6 a number of MB/MBSs were loaned to London Country to ease their vehicle shortage, while a sorry spectacle to passengers on the Midland main line out of St Pancras were the several hundred members of the class stored at Radlett Aerodrome. As could be expected, much criticism was aimed at

London Transport and the Greater London Council over the waste of such modern buses.

With the exception of the MBAs on the Red Arrow services, all Merlins in ordinary service were withdrawn by the end of 1976, with the conversion of the 235 route to SM/SMD and the 244 back to SMS operation. The MBAs were originally MBSs from the 439-615 batch and survived until replaced by LS class Leyland National 2s from April 1981. The very last in stock was MBS217, surviving with London Buses until 1987, having been allocated to the experimental shop at Chiswick. The last to operate for London Country were MBSs 415 and 424 at the end of 1980.

Many of those withdrawn were fit only for scrap. However, a number did find further service, mainly abroad, as the independent market in the UK for high capacity buses was limited. They were used in Northern Ireland by both Citybus and Ulsterbus, who amassed some 120, although a number were damaged by terrorist attack. Operators in Australia also took the Merlin, and they were also to be found working in Mauritius, Zambia, Guyana and Dubai.

Opposite top:
MB174 at Aldgate in the early 1970s, laying over from a 42 service to Camberwell Green. This vehicle had started life as Red Arrow MBA174 in September 1968, but was reclassified and reseated to 46 along with the rest of the batch during the first half of 1970. MB174 was among many buses to be exported to Australia during 1976. *V. C. Jones/IAL*

Opposite bottom:
Country Area MBS419 of Northfleet garage working a 496 journey between King's Farm Estate, Gravesend and Northfleet in October 1969. The vehicle was new in March 1969, so was less than a year old when transferred to London Country in January 1970. It was sold for scrap 10 years later. *V. C. Jones/IAL*

Top:
The last Merlins to remain in service were those on Red Arrow duties. MBA534, looking rather down at heel, leaves London Bridge for Waterloo in September 1979. *Kevin Lane*

Above right:
AA Motor Services group member Dodds of Troon bought MB629/35 in January 1977. The former was suitably painted to celebrate the Queen's Silver Jubilee later in the year. *Kevin Lane Collection*

Class SM/SMD/SMS

Chassis: AEC Swift 4MP2R
Bodywork: Marshall/ Metro-Cammell/Park Royal
Numbers: SM/SMD/SMS1-838
Total: 838
Dates new: 1969-72

The 36ft MB class, as recounted earlier, suffered manoeuvrability problems because of its long wheelbase and rear overhang. The solution to this was the 33ft 5in SM class, introduced after the delivery of MB665. The AEC AH591 11.3 litre engine of the MB was replaced by the AH505 of 8.2 litres. The initial order, placed in 1969, was for 100 vehicles: SM1-50 were bodied by Marshall and were B42F+20 standing, while SMS51-100 carried Park Royal bodywork and were B33D+34. The former were for one-man operation, with the latter fitted with automatic fare collection machines. The first of the new class were delivered from November 1969, entering service the following January on routes 160/160A from Catford, replacing RTs. The first of the SMSs, 51-61, went to New Cross for route 70.

Large orders were subsequently made for more Swifts, although not all saw service with London Transport. The Country Area was allocated Park Royal-bodied SM101-148, (B38D+18) and Metro-Cammell-bodied SM449-538 (B41D+15). However, by the time of their delivery, operations had passed to London Country Bus Services.

London Transport received the remaining buses: SMS149-223 were fitted with AFC and bodied by Marshall (B33D+34); SMS224-448 were Park Royal-bodied (also B33D+34 and fitted with AFC); while SMS539-838 carried Metro-Cammell bodies (B33D+34) and were again fitted with AFC. Delivery was complete by February 1972, with the last few, SMS835-8, going into service at Hounslow during the following month.

In May 1974, SMS75 had its AFC equipment removed and was up-seated to B42D for use as a conventional one-man bus. The new classification was SMD and, following lengthy trials, it was decided to proceed with 115 conversions, the work being carried out at Poplar garage. Park Royal-bodied SMSs were used for these conversions, from SMS51-100 and 384-448 batches. Seating replaced the AFC equipment and part of the standing area, with the centre doors being sealed but not actually removed. Work started early in 1976, although during the year the numbers to be dealt with were reduced, with only 104 having been changed by the time that the programme was ended in January 1977.

Like the Merlins before them, the Swifts were less than reliable machines and, after just 20 overhauls, the decision came to replace them as soon as possible. A three-year recertification of certain vehicles was undertaken, although heavy withdrawals were also taking place as the class was ousted by DMSs, LSs and BLs.

The decline of the class had now set in. The last SMDs were withdrawn from service in April 1978, although some survived longer as staff buses. The SMS made a slight comeback in 1979, with the delivery of LSs resulting in a surplus. Some were used on Red Arrow services in order to release MBAs for overhauls, while better availability of the type saw them replace DMSs on routes 42 and 84 in the November. The last SMs ran from Southall in September 1980, with the last SMSs surviving on Red Arrow duties until July 1981.

Many of the Swifts ended up with South Yorkshire dealers, often for scrap, while notable disposals for further service included Ulsterbus and Citybus of Belfast, with a number being exported to Malta. Several have been preserved.

Opposite top
SMS297 waiting at Uxbridge station to work a 204 to Hayes in September 1979. *Kevin Lane*

Opposite bottom:
SMD434 was converted from SMS434 in September 1976, lasting in this form until withdrawal in April 1978. Before the conversion, SMS434 is seen on a 12A — judging by the position of the camera, the photograph was taken from the open platform of an RT or RM. SMD434 later swapped the streets of south London for those of Belfast, serving with Citybus as their 72 between December 1978 and February 1980, when it was one of 19 buses destroyed by an incendiary bomb attack at the Falls Road depot. *Kevin Lane Collection*

Above:
A number of spare SMSs were allocated to Red Arrow services from July 1979. Here SMS775 works a 507 along Victoria Street in 1980. *Kevin Lane Collection*

Left:
SM449-538 were delivered straight to London Country in 1970 and 1971 and included both Park Royal and Metro-Cammell-bodied examples. When new they carried Lincoln green and canary yellow livery, superseded by NBC corporate green. An overhaul programme got under way in April 1976, although not all received a repaint, ending their days in the same livery. Dartford garage's SM514 and 517 were the last two, surviving until 1981. In September 1979, SM514 loads in Dartford running between Belvedere and Joyce Green Hospital. *Kevin Lane*

Class D/DM/DMS

Chassis: Daimler Fleetline
Bodywork: Metro-Cammell/ Park Royal
Numbers: D/DM/DMS1-2646
Total: 2,646
Dates new: 1970-78

From 1965 London Transport conducted trials between the Leyland Atlantean (XA class) and the Daimler Fleetline (XF class) with a view to operating OMO double-deckers. Although only eight of the Daimler Fleetline were operated, it was this type that was chosen to be the standard London double-decker of the 1970s and beyond. As is well known, the choice was poorly made and the type fell well short of expectations.

Delivered over eight years, between September 1970 and August 1978, the class was given three basic class codes: DMS for vehicles with a standee area, DM for crew-worked DMSs and later D for OMO DMs. Very angular bodywork was provided by Park Royal and Metro-Cammell to a similar design with only detail differences to distinguish the two (on the Metro-Cammell bodies for instance, the beading is extended above the upper-deck front windows). The Gardńer 6LXB was to be fitted as standard — but output of these engines could not keep pace with demand and the Leyland 0680 was also used extensively. Trials were also made with Rolls-Royce units and late in life the survivors received Iveco engines.

The original 1969 order for the type was for just 17 vehicles, to form an initial evaluatory batch. However, due to delivery problems, they came with the next two batches of 100 and 250, which arrived continuously during 1970-71. The first DMSs entered service in January 1971 on routes 95, 220, 271 and 189 from Brixton, Shepherds Bush, Holloway and Merton garages respectively. These buses carried Park Royal H44/24D bodies with a standee area for a further 21. Two entrance doors were provided at the front, one for passengers to pay the driver and one allowing access to use the AFC machine, centre doors providing the exit. Gardner 6LXB engines were fitted to all except DMS132, which was tried with a Leyland 0680.

With London Transport keen to replace the Routemasters and the remaining RTs by 1978, large orders for the DMS were made. The order for 1,600 planned for delivery in 1972-74 was split between Park Royal and Metro-Cammell. They were numbered DM/DMS368-1217 and 1218-1967 respectively. As the vehicles were delivered together there were numberings to catch the unwary; for instance, Park Royal-bodied DMS901 was registered SMU 901N, while Metro-Cammell bodied DMS1248 was registered JGU 248K: so high-numbered buses were not always newer! Among these vehicles were DMS864 and DM1199, both fitted with Rolls-Royce Eagle engines.

It was recognised that crew operation would still be required, so some 400 vehicles were delivered with a seat for three fitted instead of the AFC machine. These were numbered DM918-1247 and 1703-1832, the first entering service on route 16 in September 1974.

The next batch — 679 vehicles delivered during 1976-78 — turned out to be the last and were intended to oust the remaining Merlin single-deckers and RTs. The last 400 of these were of the B20 type, fitted with Leyland turbocharged engines and carrying alterations to reduce noise levels.

Below:
Park Royal-bodied DMS1-167 were easily distinguishable by the close positioning of the headlights; from DMS168 they were set further apart to aid visibility at night. DMS136 was new in June 1971, and is seen at Hampton Court station on Hammersmith-bound route 267. The 267 was converted from RM to DMS in September 1971, this view probably dating from around that time. DMS136 has latterly served as an exhibition unit with the Dyfed Fire and Rescue Service, Carmarthen. *V. C. Jones/IAL*

The first overhauls were due by 1976, but problems in separating the Park Royal body from the chassis of DMS1 led to alterations at Aldenham to deal with the vehicle as a whole. Although it was found that the Metro-Cammell bodies were detachable, it was decided to overhaul them similarly. By the time that the last of the class had arrived (DM2646 in August 1978) maintenance problems were mounting, pushing up costs to an unacceptable level. DMS251 was sold for scrap in February 1979 (when both the RT and RF classes were still, but only just, in service). The same year saw the first conversion back to Routemaster operation and the abandonment of AFC in favour of pay-as-you-enter.

Although it was downhill from then on for the class, a number were used as driver trainers, and a vehicle shortage in 1980 prompted recertifications. The decision as to which engine or body type to retain longer changed several times, although it was the B20s that were to be kept in service until the end; indeed, such was the culling of the earlier members of the class that virtually all non-B20s had gone by the end of 1983. The decision to retain the B20s led to the overhaul of those not already dealt with, and, from 1987, a programme to fit Iveco engines.

With the tendering of routes by now under way, London Buses Ltd won several contracts for which the DMS was ideal. June 1987 saw the Kingston network in operation, the DMSs being non-B20s taken from training duties, while those at Sutton in November 1988 were drawn from

Top:
St Albans, on route 84, was probably the furthest north that the London DMS would reach in normal service. This photograph shows MCW-bodied DMS1895 waiting outside St Albans London Country bus garage in June 1981 loading for Arnos Grove station. A London Country RP class AEC Reliance sits behind. The 84 began to lose its Fleetlines in favour of Metrobuses from November 1981. *Kevin Lane*

Above:
When operation of Bexleybus DMSs ceased in January 1990, four of them, DMS1160, 2109/12/43, were sent to Merton to release B20 Fleetlines for LRT tendered route 196. These retained Bexleybus blue and cream, but with the addition of a red front and were used during April and May for just two weeks. They were then replaced by Metrobuses following the conversion of the 39 to minibuses. DMS2112 is pictured outside the Arding & Hobbs store at Clapham Junction in May 1990 working a 219 towards Mitcham. *Kevin Lane Collection*

existing stock. The scheme at Bexleyheath, which commenced in January 1988, included some 14 DMSs that had previously been sold to Western SMT in 1981/83. In common with most other sold Fleetlines, they had been converted to single-door and ran as such alongside 17 resurrected London buses. They ran in an attractive blue and white colour scheme and were also renumbered in the separate Bexleybus fleet, surviving there until 1990.

Withdrawal of the B20 Fleetlines began in September 1990. The last years of the class were concentrated south of the river, with the largest allocations at garages such as Sutton, Merton, Thornton Heath and Stockwell. However, a few could be found elsewhere, often held for private hire, contracts and other odd duties. The end of regular Fleetline operation was marked by a mammoth journey from Chipstead Valley in the south, across London to Hammond Street in the north, and back with DMS2438 on 2 January 1993. A few others lingered on, including a handful of driver trainers, a total of 21 surviving to pass into privatisation.

When it was decided in 1979 to dispose of the DMS, this massive undertaking was handled by the dealer Ensign of Grays who had negotiated exclusively to buy the vehicles as they became available. These were refurbished, rebuilt or stripped for spares depending on condition, and prepared for resale. There was a ready market for large quantities of relatively modern double-deckers and the DMS soon began turning up in fleets all over the country. The traditional market for secondhand buses — the independents — was well represented by such concerns as Stevensons of Uttoxeter and Grahams of Paisley, both of which took large numbers, down to the many who operated only one or two. More notable, however, were the major operators with an eye for a bargain. These included National Bus Company, Scottish Bus Group, local authorities and PTEs including Hants & Dorset, Midland Fox, Western National, Western SMT, West Midlands PTE, Chesterfield and Grimsby-Cleethorpes.

A number ran in London with operators running tendered services under LRT contracts; indeed, the very first batch of tendered routes included the 81 (Hounslow-Slough) on which London Buslines initially used DMs. Further-more, the class had become virtually the standard London sightseeing bus during the 1980s. Many buses have ended up in a variety of non-PSV roles, while export customers have been found in Europe, the USA and, particularly, Hong Kong. Several vehicles have been preserved, including DMS1 as part of the London Transport collection at Covent Garden. The DMS is far from dead, with the last chapter still a long way off.

Opposite top
The last DMSs to see service in London were the B20s, easily distinguished by their angled vents, seen here on Sutton's DMS2489 passing Norwood Junction on a 157 in June 1990. This particular bus was still with the privatised London General in 1996, one of seven used for driver training and reclassified DMT. *Kevin Lane*

Opposite below:
The history of DMS disposals is complicated by the number of categories of operator using the type, often with more success than LT. A number ran within the National Bus Company; Midland Red (East) and its successor, Midland Fox, took over 120 since 1982. Among the first batch was former DM1812, pictured at the old St Margaret's bus station in Leicester in April 1982 in the company of another, older, Midland Red Fleetline. *Kevin Lane*

Top:
Many independents took the DMS, an ideal tool for stage, school and contract work. Lincolnshire operator Kime's of Folkingham could number several of the type in its fleet, including B20 DMS2524 acquired from London Buses in June 1992. It still looks smart passing through its home village a year later. *Kevin Lane*

Above:
Hong Kong operators have taken many DMSs, the best customers being China Motor Bus, with 206 and Kowloon Motor Bus with 100. Among the smaller operators is Argos Bus Services, formed only in 1982, whose No 23 was formerly Park Royal-bodied DMS106. *Michael Fowler*

Class LS/LSL

Chassis: Leyland National/ Leyland National 2
Bodywork: Leyland National
Numbers: LS1-506, LSL1/2
Total: 508
Dates new: 1973/76-81

The ubiquitous Leyland National entered the LT fleet as six evaluatory vehicles in 1973, when LS1-6 (TGY 101-106M) began work alongside the Metro-Scania MS class on route S2 from Dalston garage. This followed inspection of a Leyland National earlier in the year, something which led to some modifications, such as to the gearbox, before the first batch was delivered. The first six were 10.3m models, B36D+27, and were notable in having a rear route number display.

The vehicles performed satisfactorily, so much so that a cancelled export order for 51 Leyland Nationals intended for Venezuela was eagerly taken up in 1976. These buses were numbered LS7-57 and registered KJD 507-557P, entering service at Hounslow garage along with LS1-6, thus allowing the reallocation of SMSs.

As operators elsewhere were finding, the Leyland National was proving to be a reliable machine and large orders followed to replace the troublesome Swifts. Batches were delivered during 1977-79 to bring up a total of 437. It was not only Swifts that were being replaced. Notable were those sent to Kingston for routes 218 and 219 in March 1979, replacing the very last of the RFs, while others in the same year were used to allow the withdrawal of DMSs then getting under way.

It was the intention not to buy any of the Leyland National 2 models. However, during 1980 a couple of the type were inspected, Fishwick WRN 413V and Ribble DBV 841W. These preceded an order for 69 10.6m buses to replace the Red Arrow MBAs in 1981. LS438-506, registered GUW 438-506W, were all in stock by the July and were B24D+46. Fareboxes were fitted instead of the turnstiles used on the MBAs. The first of the Red Arrow LSs were put to work on the 502 and 513 routes from the new Ash Grove garage in Hackney in the April, while Gillingham Street, Victoria, received its vehicles for routes 500 and 507 in the

Below:
LS1, photographed at Hatton Cross station in July 1977 when allocated to Hounslow garage. Following withdrawal in 1985, LS1 went on to operate for Red Rover, Ensignbus and Transcity, Sidcup. *Tony Wild*

Opposite top:
In 1986 six LSs were converted to DP42F for use on express service X99 between Harlow and Basildon, an experiment that was unsuccessful and abandoned after six months. Five of these Nationals were transferred to London Coaches and prepared for use on contracts serving the Japanese School in East Acton. The five were LS27/30/76/79/435 and the latter is seen here parked near Ealing Broadway in November 1988. They were replaced by coaches during 1989. *Kevin Lane*

Opposite below:
Twenty-one LSs were painted in the red and cream livery of Harrow Buses for use on that network from November 1987. In this photograph LS346 drops off a few passengers at South Harrow station, having arrived on a 258 from Watford in March 1990. This LRT tendered route passed to Luton & District in January 1991. *Kevin Lane*

May, and Walworth completed the conversion with the 501 in June.

By 1982, however, a reduction in the Red Arrow service led to a surplus of Leyland National 2s; some, therefore, were converted to B36D and used on the P4. Subsequently, when this route was lost through tendering, they moved on to the 210. All were returned to Red Arrow service in 1987-88, although 10 were later converted to single-door and transferred to Uxbridge. LS454 was fitted out as a Mobility bus in 1984, with additional earlier LSs undergoing conversion as the network expanded. These were owned by LRT and leased to London Buses. Two later Mobility Leyland Nationals came from Southdown and Hastings Buses, numbered LSL1/2, although only the former worked for London Buses. Many of the tenders for these services were later lost by London Buses, reducing the requirement for LSs in the fleet.

Although the first standard LSs were withdrawn in 1985, they have continued in service throughout the last years of London Buses, appearing in a number of guises. Both the Harrow and

D5
ISLE OF DOGS (ASDA) &
MILE END STATION
EAST LONDON
EAST LONDON
THX 227S

171
ELEPHANT & CASTLE
SILK CUT
RED ARROW
555
RED ARROW
LEYLAND
GUW 493W
UHX 368S

Bexleybus networks had among their allocations LSs wearing the appropriate liveries. Between 1989 and 1993, 11 LSs received a special livery, incorporating gold 'East London' fleetnames and relief, seeing use on Docklands service D5.

The decline of the class has, in part, been due to the loss of work through route tendering. A particular blow was the closure of the all-LS Loughton garage in May 1986. The last ordinary LSs operated with Westlink, 38 passing to the privatised company, although a dozen were de-licensed and one, LS363, was used for driver training.

As noted above, the first withdrawals took place in 1985, with the removal of LS1-6, LS1 initially serving with Red Rover of Aylesbury — no stranger to old London buses. Many LSs have seen further service, the Leyland National being something of a standard deregulation vehicle. Well-known names have included Eastbourne Buses, Parfitt's of Rhymney Bridge, Maidstone Boro'line, Thames Transit and British Airways. Forty-two of the Leyland National 2s were refurbished by East Lancs and reclassified GLS as described later. Several others remained unrefurbished, while others have been sold.

Opposite top:
Positively gleaming in Docklands Shuttle livery, LS227 leaves the Isle of Dogs Asda store working East London route D5 in May 1990. *Kevin Lane*

Opposite below:
Red Arrow LS493 crawls along Waterloo Road in December 1985. It is working on Station Link route 555, on contract to British Rail. LS493 subsequently became the subject of a Greenway conversion. RM2074 follows on route 171. *Kevin Lane*

Above:
Nine former Red Arrow LSs were acquired by The Shires (formerly Luton & District) from Parfitt's of Rhymney Bridge in 1995. Ex-LS461 is seen in Luton, still in Parfitt's livery shortly after acquisition. *Kevin Lane*

Class MS

Chassis: Scania CR111MH
Bodywork: Metro-Cammell
Numbers: MS1-6
Total: 6
Date new: 1973

The single-deck Metro-Scania was a combination of a standard Scania Citybus married with a Metro-Cammell body. It notched up sales of just 133 between 1969 and 1974, six of which went to London Transport. VWD 451H, one of a pair of Metro-Scania demonstrators, was used at Plumstead on route 99 for three months in 1970, although it was not until 1972 that an order was made, so that the vehicle could be evaluated with the Leyland National. MS1-6 were of the CR111MH type and were registered PGC 201-206L, entering service at Dalston on the S2 in August 1973. (London Country had, incidentally, put four of the type into service at Stevenage in 1971-72.) They were used initially alongside members of the MBS class until the arrival of the LSs and remained on the S2 until June 1976 when the SMS class took over.

Although it was planned to transfer the class to Plumstead to work with the double-deck version of the type, the MD class, they were subsequently stored. MS1/3-6 were sold to Newport Transport, an enthusiastic operator of the type, and numbered 101/103-6; MS2 was kept for development use at Chiswick until November 1980 and was later secured for preservation. Of the Newport vehicles, MS1 was dismantled for spares, MS3 was sold to the Gwent Constabulary in 1991, MS4 also passed into preservation in 1991, MS5 went to the Fire Service College, Moreton-in-Marsh, again in 1991, while MS6 was scrapped following a depot fire in 1983.

Below:
Clapton Pond is the location of MS5 on route S2 in April 1975, one of the four MSs that were sold to Newport Corporation in November 1978. *G. R. Mills*

Bottom:
Former MS5 in service in Newport in August 1983. *Kevin Lane*

Class BS

Chassis: Bristol LHS6L
Bodywork: Eastern Coach Works
Numbers: BS1-17
Total: 17
Dates new: 1975-6

Following the use of FS class Ford Transits on a number of new routes, it was found that their capacity was in some cases too small. A replacement was sought and several types were inspected: Devon General 93 (VOD 93K), a Bristol LHS6L with Marshall 33-seat bodywork and SELNEC 1711 (XVU 341M), a Seddon Pennine IV with Seddon 23-seat bodywork, were loaned in June 1973, while in 1974 Seddon Pennine IV demonstrator PBU 951M carrying Seddon 25-seat bodywork was used on the C11. However, the type finally chosen was the Bristol LHS with Eastern Coach Works 26-seater bodies. These buses were unusual in having manual transmission, rare on full-sized buses in London. Furthermore, the bodies were only 24ft long, over 2ft shorter than all other ECW bodies on Bristol LHS chassis — with the exception of six that were delivered to West Yorkshire PTE at about the same time.

The first six of the class, BS1-6, were registered GHV 501-506N and entered service on the C11 in August 1975, replacing members of the FS class. A second batch of 11, BS7-17 registered OJD 7-17R, was delivered during the autumn of 1976, this time replacing FS class vehicles on the B1, P4 and W9. Earlier in 1976, the first of the longer BL class had appeared on the streets and later members were to take over the duties of the BS class, beginning with Bromley local route B1 in April 1978. The class finally bowed out of service in July 1981 with the conversion of the W9 to BL operation.

As may be expected, these useful little vehicles readily found new owners following disposal by London Transport. Subsequent operators included Busways, Newcastle, British Caledonian Airways and Western National. The type was also represented on the Isles of Scilly and on Guernsey, in the latter case, with a number of the BL class as well.

Above:
Busways, Newcastle, acquired former BS7/8 from Star Travel, Dipton, in 1988. BS7, as Busways 1612, is seen in Blue Bus Services livery approaching Gateshead Metro Centre in November 1989.
Kevin Lane

Below:
BS8 working on former FS route P4 in Brixton in May 1977. This vehicle later saw service with Busways, Newcastle, along with BS7.
Michael Fowler

Class MD

Chassis: Scania BR111DH
Bodywork: Metro-Cammell
Numbers: MD1-164
Total: 164
Dates new: 1975-77

In 1973 London Transport placed the single-deck MS class into service and in the same year the double-deck MCW Metropolitan was launched. The chassis was adapted from that used on the single-decker, the selling point being the lack of noise from the Scania power unit. The Metropolitan demonstrator, NVP 533M, was duly inspected by London Transport on several occasions between 1973 and 1975, eventually resulting in an order for 164 vehicles which were delivered between December 1975 and February 1977, the largest order for the model. MD1-164 were registered KJD 201-83P and OUC 84-164R, being of Scania BR111D type and fitted with MCW H43/29D bodywork. Like the single-deckers, the MD class were immediately distinguished by the asymmetric windscreen arrangement.

The class was introduced initially on the 36 group of routes together with the 53 and 63 from New Cross and Peckham; they were allocated to garages in south London throughout their lives and all ended up at the new Plumstead garage, which opened in October 1981, settling down to a fairly reliable existence. However, before long, with a general reduction in services, the class was inevitably declared non-standard; replacement with T class Leyland Titans started in September 1982 and was completed in June 1983 with MD127 bowing out at the Plumstead garage open day.

Many of the class found new homes after withdrawal. Reading took 21 to join others of the type bought new, while Whippet of Fenstanton bought no fewer than 17. MD1 has been preserved at the Scania Museum in Sweden.

Left:
MD101 leads a trio of the type in York Way, outside King's Cross station, in September 1979. The buses are working on route 63, which they operated from October 1976 until September 1982. *Kevin Lane*

Below:
G. & G. Coaches of Leamington Spa has operated a number of MDs, including MD16 seen at work in Coventry in November 1987. *Kevin Lane*

Class BL

Chassis: Bristol LH6L
Bodywork: Eastern Coach Works
Numbers: BL1-95
Total: 95
Dates new: 1976-77

At the time that London Transport was evaluating vehicles as a possible replacement for the FS class (it turned out to be the Bristol LHS), a Bristol LH with Eastern Coach Works bodywork from Hants & Dorset was inspected with a view to it replacing certain RF duties where width restrictions were in force, the LH being only 7ft 6in wide. This was no doubt satisfactory as 95 of the vehicles were ordered, the first entering service in April 1976 from Romford's North Street garage. The first 92 were registered KJD 401-440P (BL1-40) and OJD 41-92R (BL41-92). The last three, OJD 93-95R (BL93-95), were used to begin route 128 for the London Borough of Hillingdon and received a revised livery of red and yellow (rather than white) for the service which commenced in September 1977. These three vehicles were unusual in having an offside indicator over the first passenger window along with various other features including a transmitter which enabled the driver to raise the barrier at Mount Vernon Hospital.

The class was put to work mainly in the suburban areas of the capital, gradually ousting the smaller BS class and the RFs — the latter by now dwindling fast, although the last RFs (at Kingston) were actually replaced by LS class Leyland Nationals in March 1979. A repaint programme began in 1979 with BL4 emerging without the white window surrounds, but with a white band at waist level; even this was subsequently omitted. In 1981 Hillingdon BL94 was modified following fire damage, seating being downgraded from 39 to 29 with room for 19 standing. A bolder application of the livery, with more yellow, was also revealed. BL93 and 95 were similarly treated.

Service reductions and conversion to larger types saw a number of BL casualties during 1982, so that by the beginning of 1983 the class was operating only on five routes: the 128 from Uxbridge, the 251 from Edgware and lettered routes B1, C11 and W9 from Croydon, Holloway and Enfield respectively. On a more positive note, 1982 saw the entry into passenger service of BL2 at Edgware; it had been a training bus since new. Furthermore, BL36 and BL81 were fitted with dual-purpose seating in 1986-7.

Although the last BLs were withdrawn from passenger service in January 1991 (working from Edgware on the 251), the class was deemed useful as driver trainers, a number surviving in this role. Fifteen of these, BL1/2/4/28/34-6/49/57/65/69/78/81/85 and 91, passed with CentreWest into privatisation. Earlier disposals went to such operators as OK Motors, Bishop Auckland, Tally Ho!, Kingsbridge and Guernseybus.

Top:
BL95 loads in Ruislip High Street on Hillingdon local route 128, although the blind display is not all that it could be. The date is December 1987, the BLs on this service being replaced by LS class Leyland Nationals in the following July. BL95 later served with independent operator, South Lancs Transport of St Helens. *Kevin Lane*

Above:
Carrying a Leyland badge rather than one for a Bristol LH, BL79 works on a route 251 journey through Whetstone in September 1989. *Kevin Lane*

Left:
Robson of Thornaby acquired BL21 in 1989 and used it on local services in Cleveland, in this case between Stockton High Street and the Hardwick Estate where it is seen in January 1991. *Kevin Lane*

Class V

Chassis: Volvo Ailsa B55
Bodywork: Alexander/ Van Hool McArdle
Numbers: V1-65
Total: 65
Dates new: 1976-77/1984

The Routemasters were not the last front-engined double-deckers to be bought by London Transport. The Volvo Ailsa B55 became available in 1973, providing an option for those disenchanted with buses with the engine at the back. London Transport bought its first three at the end of the production run, V1/2 entering service in April 1984 and V3 in March 1985. They were ordered as part of the Alternative Vehicle Evaluation trials, the first two carrying Alexander R type 72-seat bodywork. V3 was rather different (explaining its lateness into service) in having a rear rather than a central exit and a rear staircase; it seated only 64, running in service as a crewed vehicle. The routes chosen for the trials were the 170 on weekdays and the 44 on Sundays, although the 77A was chosen for V3.

The three were later banished to Potters Bar where V1/2 entered service in December 1986. V3, modified by removing the rear exit but retaining the extra staircase, followed suit in February 1987.

At about this time, a batch of Volvo Ailsas was acquired from South Yorkshire PTE, 12, numbered V4-15, arriving for service at Potters Bar during 1987. One other, V16, was acquired for spares. These were notable in having bodywork by Van Hool McArdle, a short-lived joint Belgian and Irish venture. Further Volvos were acquired, this time from West Midlands Travel in 1987-88, for operation at Potters Bar and Harrow, the latter for services won by tender. They all carried Alexander AV type bodywork and were numbered V17-65.

Withdrawal of the acquired Volvos began in 1989, as they were replaced by Metrobuses. The last of these ran at Harrow, with a number seeing further service with Black Prince of Morley and Skills of Nottingham among others. Several have been preserved. Of the three trial vehicles, V1/2 survived to pass to the privatised London Northern, bought by MTL in October 1994, while V3, withdrawn following an accident in 1992, also ended up with Black Prince which embarked upon an ambitious rebuild.

Top:
Originally built with a rear door and staircase and with an H36/28D seating arrangement, V3 was rebuilt to H38/30F and entered service as such in February 1987, being allocated to Potters Bar to join V1/2. It is seen here passing High Barnet underground station two months later on route 84 (New Barnet station-St Albans), a service contracted out by Hertfordshire County Council. *Kevin Lane*

Left:
Also working the 84, this time towards New Barnet, is a former West Midlands Travel Volvo Ailsa V16, stuck in traffic in St Peter's Street, St Albans in April 1988. Others of this batch were in Harrow Bus livery. *Kevin Lane*

Class T

Chassis: Leyland Titan TN
Bodywork: Park Royal/Leyland
Numbers: T1-1131
Total: 1,131
Dates new: 1978-84

The integrally constructed Leyland Titan was intended to be the manufacturer's standard double-deck bus of the 1980s, but it sadly fell well short of the mark. London was by far its best customer, with Greater Manchester's mere 15 a very distant second.

The fourth Titan prototype, 04 (NHG 732P), was developed for London Transport and was trialled from Chalk Farm garage on routes 24 and 3 from May 1976, although at this stage it was known as the B15. Prototype 05 (BCK 706R) was also put to work on routes 24 and 3 from early 1978. From these demonstrations an initial order was placed for 50 of the type, the first arriving in 1978.

The first six of the class, designated T but originally to have been TN, entered service at Hornchurch garage in December 1978. The first 250 were built at the former AEC plant at Southall and at Park Royal. However, problems at the latter saw production eventually switched to Workington, although an intermediate batch, T251-63, contained some Park Royal parts. Full production got under way again in May 1981. Most vehicles were fitted with Gardner 6LXB units, although a few received Leyland engines for comparative trials. T369 had its hydraulic brakes changed in favour of air, with others of the class being similarly converted.

The class became common at garages throughout south and east London, interesting variations including several that received the Bexleybus blue and white livery. In 1984 the five Titans bought by the West Midlands PTE were acquired by London Transport. Registered WDA 1-5T, they became T1126-30 and after use as trainers, received coach seating for use on the 177 Express route and private hire duties. A further acquisition was that of the former demonstrator BCK 706R, which had appeared in London in 1978. It came from Fishwick, Leyland and became T1131, operating with Selkent. A major shift in operations occurred in 1990 when Westlink gained route 131 (Wimbledon-West Molesey) by tender from London & Country in the September. This required a weekday allocation of 10 double-deckers and this was satisfied by the transfer of 13 Titans from Camberwell (with the same number arriving at Camberwell from Finchley).

Apart from a few vehicles lost by fire, the first withdrawal took place in October 1992, when T277 was sold to fellow London operator, BTS. Since then many have been sold, notably to Merseybus, which has taken a large number since November 1992. At privatisation, Titans were operated by Selkent, East London, London Central, Westlink, Leaside and South London, although in single figures in the case of the last two.

Below:
T2 working a 174 journey towards Noak Hill along South Street, Romford, in November 1990. T2 duly passed to Stagecoach East London in September 1994. *Kevin Lane*

Top:
Walthamstow's T327 waiting in Ilford in November 1987 on the 123, a route that passed to Ensign Citybus in 1991. Loading behind is an Ensign DMS, formerly DMS325, working on a Dagenham-Redbridge 145, a route that subsequently returned to London Buses in June 1991, Titan-operated from Barking. T327 passed to the privatised London Central in October 1994, while DMS325 is sadly no more. *Kevin Lane*

Above:
Westlink T375 at work in Wimbledon on the 131 in December 1990, still carrying London Forest identity. *Kevin Lane*

Top:
Former West Midlands PTE T1130 on private hire duties at Brighton in September 1990, operating from Selkent's Plumstead garage. T1130 passed to the privatised Selkent in 1994, as did sister vehicles T1126/27. *Kevin Lane*

Above:
Nottingham City Transport bought T81/119 in 1993, numbering them 60/61. The latter is seen near Broadmarsh bus station in July 1995. The pair later joined the fleet of Kinch, Barrow upon Soar, itself an operator of former London Titans. *Kevin Lane*

Class M

Chassis: MCW Metrobus
Bodywork: MCW/Alexander
Numbers: M1-1485
Total: 1,485
Dates new: 1978-88

After the Metropolitan came the much more successful Metrobus, the first bus to be designed and built completely by MCW. London Transport was its biggest customer (as indeed was the case with the Metropolitan), although West Midlands PTE ran LT a close second. With all of the MD class of Metropolitans in service, the Metrobus demonstrator TOJ 592S was loaned to LT at the end of 1977; the resulting trial batch of five vehicles appeared in London in 1978-79. Numbered M1-5 and registered THX 101-5S, these vehicles were powered by Gardner 6LXB units and carried MCW H43/28D bodies. They were easily distinguishable from subsequent vehicles by the smaller destination display and the separate position for the route number. This batch entered service from Cricklewood garage on routes 16/16A working as crew-operated buses.

The type was progressively introduced during 1979-80 beginning at Fulwell and entering service in large numbers

Below:
The first five pre-production Metrobuses had smaller blind-boxes in order to take DMS type blinds. This is evident on M3 at Brent Cross in July 1984, in all-over red livery, having lost the white upper-deck window surrounds on its first overhaul. M1-5 all passed to the privatised Metroline in October 1994 along with over 150 other members of the class. *Kevin Lane*

Bottom:
M804 was converted to single-door and open-top following an accident. It is seen as such working for London Northern on seasonal route Z1 (Baker Street-London Zoo) in May 1994.
P. R. Wallis

throughout north, west and south-west London, replacing in the main DMS and single-deck types. From November 1980 the type was introduced on Airbus services A1 and A2, linking Heathrow Airport with Victoria and Paddington respectively. For this, M431-47 were converted to H43/9D allowing a large area of luggage space in the lower saloon. Destination blinds were white on blue. Subsequent conversions included M1006-29 which also boasted wheelchair lifts. Other members of the class were recruited to the service to act as extra vehicles during the summer months. Metrobuses continued to work Airbus services until replaced by Volvo Olympians during 1995.

While the delivery of the 1,440 standard Metrobuses was in hand, a pair of the Mk II models were purchased to take part in trials with Leyland Olympian, Dennis Dominator and Volvo B55 types in 1985. The Mk II was launched in 1982 and contained considerably fewer body parts and lacked the asymmetric windscreen of the Mk I. The two Mk IIs were numbered M1441/42 (A441/42 UUV), the former being powered by the Gardner 6LXB, the latter by a Cummins L10. There

Above:
M1010, one of the Metrobuses dedicated to Airbus duties, seen at Heathrow in October 1984. *Kevin Lane*

Below:
Four single-doored Metrobuses were acquired from Greater Manchester in 1987, including former 5009 which became M1447 with London Buses. It is seen on route W8 at Edmonton in August 1987. *Kevin Lane*

Above:
Also in 1987 at Edmonton Green on a W8 journey is M1451, one of four Ms that came from Yorkshire Rider. More ordinary M353 stands behind in this August 1987 view. *Kevin Lane*

Below:
Two of the Yorkshire Rider acquisitions featured Alexander RH type bodywork, illustrated here on M1449 allocated to Potters Bar on a 234 from Archway to Barnet in June 1990. *Kevin Lane*

should have been a third, to be M1443, which was planned as a prototype for a Mk3 Metrobus; in the event it was never completed and the Mk3 never got off the ground. The only Mk IIs to be acquired subsequently were M1452-80 (E452-78 SON, E479/80 UOF), single-doored buses for use at Harrow, and were painted in Harrow Buses' red and cream livery. They went into service from November 1987 and remained there until the loss of the contract in January 1991 when they were returned off lease.

The other members of the Metrobus fleet were a few bought secondhand for tendered routes in 1987-88, initially entering service at Potters Bar. Greater Manchester supplied M1443-47 (GBU 1/4/5/8/9V); M1448-51 (UWW 518/9X and CUB 539/40Y) came from Yorkshire Rider; and M1481-85 (VRG 415-19T) came from Busways. All carried MCW bodies with the exception of M1448/49, which were bodied by Alexander.

The Harrow Metrobuses soon found new homes, including Reading Transport, Capital Citybus and the Manchester independent Finglands. The first of the other Metrobuses were withdrawn in 1993, including ex-Tyne & Wear M1481-4, all passing to Merseybus, which was then buying large numbers of Titans from London Buses. However, for the time being at least, sales of Metrobuses have ceased. At privatisation there were Metrobuses represented with CentreWest, Leaside, Metroline, London General, London Northern, London United and South London.

Above:
Mk II Metrobuses M1452-80 were leased by London Buses between 1987-88 and 1990-91 for use in the Harrow area, receiving an attractive livery of red and cream. M1452 unloads at Burnt Oak underground station working route 114 between Ruislip and Mill Hill Broadway station in November 1990. Following its return off lease, it passed to Great Yarmouth Transport along with M1453/5. *Kevin Lane*

Below:
The Great Yarmouth trio were numbered 59-61; 61, former M1455, is seen at work in the town centre in August 1993. *Kevin Lane*

Class H

Chassis: Hestair-Dennis Dominator
Bodywork: Northern Counties
Numbers: H1-3
Total: 3
Date new: 1984

Three Hestair-Dennis Dominators took part in the Alternative Vehicle Evaluation trials alongside the Leyland Olympian, Volvo Ailsa and Mk II Metrobus types. H1-3 were delivered in November 1984, entering service during the following year. The buses were registered B101-103 WUW and were powered by Gardner 6LXB engines with Maxwell (H1) or Voith (H2/3) gearboxes. Northern Counties dual-door bodies were fitted, similar in style to those operating with Greater Manchester. Following their use on trial routes 170 and 44, they were taken out of service in September 1986, although they eventually ended up working from Brixton garage by the summer of 1987.

In October 1991 the three passed to London Coaches, set up in 1986 and privatised in May 1992.

Above:
The first of the Dennis Dominators to enter service was H3, on 4 February 1985. It is seen here at West Hampstead having arrived on a 159 from Streatham, working from Brixton garage. The type was introduced onto this route on Sundays only from January 1990, being RM/RML-worked during the week. *Kevin Lane Collection*

Left:
A comparative view of H3 with London Coaches, in which several detail differences can be detected, not least the removal of the fog lamps. The location is Victoria; the date, February 1994. *Kevin Lane*

Class L

Chassis: Leyland Olympian
Bodywork: Eastern Coach Works/Northern Counties/ Leyland/Alexander
Numbers: L1-354
Total: 354
Dates new: 1984/1986-89/1992

The Leyland Olympian was built at Bristol from 1978, although by the time that London Transport took an interest, production had switched to Workington and the vehicle had become Leyland's standard double-decker. Three were ordered as part of the Alternative Vehicle Evaluation trials, to be tried against the Mk II Metrobus, Dennis Dominator and Volvo Ailsa largely on routes 170 and 44. The trio arrived early in 1984, numbered L1-3 and registered A101-3 SYE. All of the three carried bodywork by Eastern Coach Works, although L1 was fitted with a Leyland TL11 engine and Hydracyclic gearbox, while L2/3 were powered by the Gardner 6LXB in conjunction with a Voith gearbox. Following the trials, the decision was made to order a further 260 Olympians, with Gardner engines and Voith gearboxes.

The vehicles began to arrive early in 1986, the first entering service in the March. They were steadily allocated to garages south of London, with delivery completed within a year. Notable

Right:
ECW-bodied L38 at Orpington station in August 1986 on a route 51 working from Woolwich. Later in the month, the service became an LRT tendered route, passing to London Country, and subsequently to Kentish Bus. L38 was with South London when the company was privatised in December 1994. *Kevin Lane*

Below:
Carrying London Central Travel livery and the registration from RM1002, L261 sits in the rain in the coach park at Bognor Regis in May 1994, having brought a party from Slade Green. London Central passed to the Go-Ahead Group in October of the same year, and L261 went with it. *Kevin Lane*

BROMLEY NORTH STN
Parkhill Road Hurst Road
269
This is an AUTOCHECK Bus
BUS
E914 KYR
BUS STOP

237
Chiswick Brentford
Hounslow Feltham
SUNBURY VILLAGE
RIVERSIDEBUS
Leyland
G307 UYK

amongst this batch were L166-71 and L260-3 which received coach seating for limited stop and private hire work.

A further batch of 28 Olympians was leased for use on the Bexleybus network, and entered service in January 1988. These buses were built to full Greater Manchester specification, having been diverted from that operator, and carried Northern Counties bodywork. Gardner engines with Hydracyclic gearboxes were fitted, the vehicles being finished in the attractive Bexleybus blue and cream livery. They became L264-91, although they also received Bexleybus numbers 1-28, and were registered E901-28 KYR.

L292-314 were Leyland Olympians ordered specifically for tendered route 237 (Shepherds Bush-Sunbury Village), which commenced on 6 January 1990. Powered by Cummins engines, they had Leyland bodywork to similar style — though single-door — to the earlier ECW bodies. The last three, L312-4, were fitted with coach seats and were later used on the short-lived Airbus route A3 to Stansted Airport.

The last Leyland Olympians were L315-54, Alexander-bodied examples for Leaside at Stamford Hill, which began replacing Leyland Titans and some Metrobuses from March 1992. The last four of these had coach seating.

With the advent of privatisation at the end of 1994, all of the Leyland Olympians, with the exception of Northern Counties-bodied L264-91, went to five of the new companies: Selkent, London Central, Leaside, London United and South London. The former Bexleybus vehicles were returned off lease following the loss of the contract of the services by Selkent. They were replaced by Titans of London Central, the new operator, from November 1990. The youthful Olympians subsequently travelled far and wide, including Liverpool and Newcastle, while three made it to Sentosa, an island off Singapore! Further Volvo-built Olympians were later to enter service with various ex-London Buses companies after privatisation, under a variety of class names.

Opposite top:
Northern Counties-bodied L277, one of the Bexleybus Olympians, loading in Bexleyheath on a 269 service bound for Bromley North station in January 1988, the first month of the scheme's operation. The 269 was taken over by Kentish Bus three years later, while L277 became one of 21 of the batch to pass to Busways, Newcastle, in 1991. *Kevin Lane*

Opposite below:
All-Leyland L307 passing through Isleworth on its way to Sunbury Village in June 1991. *Kevin Lane*

Below:
Alexander-bodied L333 stands at Euston station in June 1993 on a 253 journey to Hackney Central. This is the only one of the batch with a registration number not matching its fleet number. *Andrew Lane*

Class C

Chassis: Volvo Citybus
Bodywork: Alexander
Number: C1
Total: 1
Date new: 1985

In 1985 London Buses leased an Alexander-bodied Volvo Citybus, an underfloor-engined double-decker based on Volvo's B10M single-deck chassis. Registered C101 CUL and given the number C1, the vehicle was on loan to trial its unique feature, a Volvo Flygmotor Cumulo drive system. This converted braking energy (usually lost as heat) into accelerating energy. Advantages to this system included less transmission and brake wear and tear, fewer exhaust emissions and a significant saving on fuel.

The leasing arrangement began in August 1985, although the bus did not enter service until July 1986, from Palmers Green garage, working on route 102, Golders Green to Chingford. Following its trials, C1 was delicensed in September 1987 and returned to Volvo. It later appeared in the fleet of West Yorkshire independent operator, Black Prince of Morley, its Cumulo system replaced by a conventional ZF automatic gearbox. However, it involved a complex hydrostatic drive and very high-pressure hydraulic systems, of which the technical difficulties are yet to be ironed out.

Left:
C1 finally entered service in July 1986. It is seen here at Golders Green working from Palmers Green garage on a 102 to Chingford, normally a Metrobus duty. *Ian Cowley*

Below:
C1 later served with Black Prince, Morley, acquired in March 1989 from McMenemy of Ardrossan, part of A1 Services. *Michael Fowler*

Class LX

Chassis: Leyland Lynx
Bodywork: Leyland
Numbers: LX1-11
Total: 11
Dates new: 1988-89

The rear-engined semi-integral Leyland Lynx appeared in 1985 as the replacement for the Leyland National. Several of the independent operators in the capital have used the type, although London Buses ran only a small number. The first two, LX1/2 registered F101/2 GRM, were in fact owned by the London Borough of Hillingdon and were used to replace the LSs then in use on route 128/128A. They received the red, yellow and grey Hillingdon livery and entered service in February 1989. Cummins engines were fitted, while seating was split between 33 bus and 14 dual-purpose.

Six further Lynxes entered service in September 1989, this time with London United on route 283 (Hammersmith-East Acton), a tendered service formerly operated by Scancoaches. LX3-8 were registered G73-78 UYV and were again fitted with Cummins engines.

Three more Lynxes were acquired late in 1989, former Merthyr Tydfil Transport D105/6/11 NDW, new in 1987, for service at Hillingdon on the 128/128A, where they became LX9-11. They were later re-registered 809-811 DYE, formerly carried by Routemasters RM1809-11 (which subsequently became the rather anonymous EBY 257/247B and EGF 220B respectively).

The London Borough of Hillingdon routes 128/128A were withdrawn in August 1991, the five Lynxes staying at Uxbridge where they were used on the 607 Express route between Uxbridge and Shepherds Bush, together with ex-Red Arrow LSs.

On privatisation, LX1/2/9-11 were still with CentreWest, while LX3-8 passed to London United.

Above:
LX1 in full Hillingdon livery leaves Ruislip station for Harefield Hospital in April 1990. *Kevin Lane*

Below:
LX2 in 607 Express livery heading through Southall towards Uxbridge in November 1991. This vehicle was later re-registered 292 CLT.
R. J. Waterhouse

Class DA

Chassis: DAF SB220
Bodywork: Optare
Numbers: DA1-35

Total: 35
Dates new: 1989-92

The DAF Optare Delta is a UK version of the Dutch DAF SB220 Citybus and has proved reasonably popular with operators in this country since 1988. It is powered by an 11.6 litre DAF rear engine. London Buses took an interest early in 1989, with demonstrator F370 BUA used from Plumstead garage on route 180 in the March. DA1, registered F54 CWY but later becoming WLT 400, joined Selkent at Bromley in the June. It was a dual-purpose 49-seater rather than the 53-seat bus that was demonstrated. Two-doored DA2, registered F551 SHX, went into Red Arrow service later in the year, but was later converted to single-door and transferred to Westlink. DA3-9, registered G931-7 MYG, went to Westlink from April 1990 to operate on tendered route 110 (Twickenham-Cranford) formerly operated by London & Country.

A further demonstrator, G684 KNW, was used by East London at Seven Kings garage during 1991, being taken into stock in the July as DA10. The resulting order saw the arrival of DA11-29, registered J711-29 CYG, in 1992 for use on the 129 and 148 routes at Seven Kings. These dual-door buses follow the time-honoured tradition of being to a special design for London, with a specially raised floor in the forward half of the vehicle, on which is a standee area, eliminating the need for the double step over the rear axle of the standard Delta. Further members of the class for East London were DA30-35, registered K630-35 HWX, delivered late in 1992.

Privatisation saw DA1-9 in the Westlink fleet, while DA10-35 passed to Stagecoach-owned East London.

Below:
DA2 was the second of the DAF-Optare Deltas and was completed to Red Arrow specifications as B30D+52. It is seen in this guise at Victoria, late in 1989. *Kevin Lane Collection*

Opposite top:
Following its conversion to single-door, DA2 went to Westlink. It is seen at Hounslow before working a 110 journey to Twickenham in December 1990. *Kevin Lane*

Opposite below:
DA13, one of the East London Deltas, in Green Lane, Ilford, on its way to Romford Market in June 1992. *R. J. Waterhouse*

B
WESTLINK
DAF
F551 SHX

Gants Hill Ilford
Green Lane Becontree Heath
ROMFORD MARKET
129
AP 16
EAST LONDON
DA 13
EAST LONDON
OPTARE
J713 CYG

Class RN

Chassis: Renault PR100/2
Bodywork: Northern Counties
Number: RN1
Total: 1
Date new: 1989

Above:
RN1 at Romford in February 1991 working a route 86 to Ilford, when operating from Seven Kings garage. *G. R. Mills*

The Renault PR100, seen in large numbers across the Channel, has failed to succeed in the UK. A demonstrator, F100 AKB with Northern Counties single-door 51-seat bodywork, was trialled at Seven Kings in March/April 1989 with East London, working on route 150. A single, similar vehicle was brought in for evaluation against DAF Optare Delta and Scania types. Numbered RN1 and registered G276 VML, the bus went to Seven Kings, again for the 150, from November 1989, moving on to Stamford Hill in April 1990, but returning later to Seven Kings.

RN1 was withdrawn and sold in 1993 to Hornsby of Scunthorpe, joining the former demonstrator F100 AKB (by then registered WUK 155) in that fleet.

Class SA

Chassis: Scania N113CRB
Bodywork: Alexander
Number: SA1
Total: 1
Date new: 1989

The single Scania N113CRB was delivered to Thornton Heath garage in August 1989. It carried Alexander 51-seat bodywork and as such was the first single-deck Scania in the fleet since the MS class of 1973. It was numbered SA1 and was registered F113 OMJ. After a spell of driver training it went into service in the October on route 59, Brixton to Purley, passing to Bromley in exchange for DA1 in the following February. Although it returned to Thornton Heath in the June, it went back to Scania in October, not having proved a success.

Below:
SA1 outside Thornton Heath garage in August 1989, shortly after delivery, before being used for driver training. *Bill Godwin*

Right:
SA1 put in an appearance at Showbus 1989, as seen here on 24 August. *Kevin Lane*

Class S

Chassis: Scania N112DRB	**Numbers:** S1-71
Bodywork: Alexander/ Northern Counties	**Total:** 71
	Dates new: 1989/91-2

The first nine of this class, S1-9 registered F421-29 GWG, were acquired for specific use by London Northern on LRT tendered route 263 (Archway station-Barnet General Hospital) from July 1989. Alexander R type single-door bodywork was fitted, these buses replacing acquired single-door Metrobuses.

The second batch, S10-29 registered J810-29 HMC and with similar Alexander bodywork, were delivered in late 1991 for Docklands Light Railway replacement services, operated by East London from West Ham garage and replacing Leyland Titans.

The rest of the class carried Northern Counties single-door bodywork and were numbered S30-71 and registered J230/1 XKY, J132-45 HMT and K846-71 LMK. S30/31 went to Potters Bar in December 1991, with the balance entering service with East London during 1992. S30/31 had gone east earlier in 1992, in exchange for two of the Alexander-bodied vehicles, while a further nine of this batch passed from East London to London Northern later in the year to initiate 'Red Express X43', a limited stop peak-hour service from North Finchley to London Bridge which began on 3 August, in conjunction with the first 'Red Route' traffic scheme. By privatisation, London Northern had S1-21 with the rest all with East London, owned by MTL and Stagecoach respectively.

Right:
London Northern S3 at work on the LRT tendered route for which the first nine were bought, the 263 (Barnet General Hospital-Archway). The location is the High Road, Whetstone, and the date is September 1989.
Kevin Lane

Below:
Representing the Northern Counties-bodied batches is East London's S71 seen at Waterloo in 1993, working from Bow garage on route 26, on which it has replaced Leyland Titans.
Kevin Lane

Class VC

Chassis: Volvo Citybus B10M-50
Bodywork: Northern Counties
Numbers: VC1-39
Total: 39
Dates new: 1989-90/91

Two batches of Northern Counties-bodied Volvo Citybuses were put into service by London General at Stockwell following successful LRT route tendering. VC1-27, registered G101-27 NGN, were put to work on the 133 (Liverpool Street station-Tooting Broadway) from January 1990, while VC28-38, registered G128-38 PGK, were used on the 196 (Norwood Junction-Brixton) from April 1990. A further VC was delivered at the end of 1991 and registered J139 DGF, although this, along with a number of others of the class, has subsequently received Routemaster registrations. All passed to the privatised London General in October 1994.

Below:
VC1-3 were delivered with coach seating on the upper deck and bus seating on the lower. This made them more suitable for private hire duties, demonstrated here by VC2 at Brighton in September 1990.
Kevin Lane

Bottom:
VC6, one of the first batch, standing at London Bridge station before heading for Tooting Broadway in May 1990. It later received the registration from RM60, VLT 60. *Kevin Lane*

Class DK

Chassis: DAF SB220LC
Bodywork: Ikarus
Numbers: DK1-10
Total: 10
Date new: 1992

Former Green Line route 726 was put out to competitive tender by London Transport in 1991. The route, from Heathrow Airport to Dartford, was formerly operated by Kentish Bus and Luton & District and was due to be withdrawn with other Green Line routes from June 1991 when London Transport withdrew its subsidies. Protests from local councils served by the route saw its reappraisal and tendering, the new operator being London Coaches, who took over in February 1992.

The new vehicles for the service, rebranded as 726 Expresslink, were Ikarus-bodied DAF SB220s, seating 44 to dual-purpose specification. There were 10 vehicles, numbered DK1-10 and registered J801-10 KHD. Seat belts were fitted to the first two rows of seats — a London first — conforming to EC regulations for coaches. A new livery of red, white and grey helped to establish the new image.

The operation of these vehicles within London Buses was brief, as London Coaches were privatised in the May. Three further vehicles, DK11-13 (L511-13 KJX), were added in 1994. They were also the first London buses bodied in Hungary, a fact demonstrated by the carrying of 'H'-plates on their rear ends!

Below:
DK2 loading for Dartford in Bexleyheath, shortly after the start of the new service. *Kevin Lane Collection*

Class LA

Chassis: Dennis Lance **Total:** 16
Bodywork: Alexander **Date new:** 1992
Numbers: LA1-16

The rear-engined Dennis Lance was introduced in 1991 to complete Dennis's range of single-deck types. The first to enter service in Britain were in London as the LA class, fitted with Cummins C-series engines, ZF automatic transmission and Alexander PS 39-seat, dual-door bodies. LA1-16, registered J101-10/411/112-116, were put onto the 36B route from May 1992 from Catford garage, replacing Routemasters. All passed to Stagecoach on privatisation in September 1994 and were expected to leave London for Ribble at Bolton in 1997.

Above:
LA1 in the rain at Peckham on a Camberwell Green-bound 36B in December 1993. *P. R. Wallis*

Class GLS

Chassis: Leyland National 2
Bodywork: Leyland, rebuilt East Lancs
Numbers: GLS1/2, GLS438-506 (with gaps)
Total: 43
Dates rebuilt: 1992-4

In order to extend the life of a Leyland National to up to 10 years, the bodybuilders East Lancs developed the National Greenway refurbishment package. This incorporated a complete restyling, new panels (losing that characteristic riveted finish) and interior, and a different choice of engine if required.

The pilot conversion for London Buses was carried out on LS466, a Red Arrow vehicle for London General, this becoming GLS1. The second conversion was on an 11.6m National, the former North Western and before that Crosville FCA 9X. Unlike the dual-doored GLS1, GLS2 was to single-door dual-purpose specification. GLS1 entered service on Red Arrow duties in December 1992, while GLS2 had gone to work on the 607 Express from Uxbridge in the October. Its original registration was changed to 292 CLT in February 1993.

A further 41 Red Arrow-type Leyland National 2s were converted during 1993-4 and numbered GLS438-40/2/3/6/8-50/2/5/9/60/3/7-9/71/3/4/6-81/3/6/7/90-3/6/8-502/5/6.

All of these, together with GLS1, passed to the privatised London General, while GLS2 went to CentreWest. Their original Leyland O.680H engines were replaced by Gardner 6HLXBs, the standard engine for Greenway. Doubt about Gardner's future meant that the order was changed to DAF — which promptly went into receivership, so Gardner won through in the end!

Below:
GLS469 working a London Bridge-bound 501 at Waterloo during the summer of 1994. *Kevin Lane*

Class SP

Chassis: DAF DB250
Bodywork: Optare Spectra
Numbers: SP1-25
Total: 25
Dates new: 1992-93

The impressive Optare Spectra was launched in 1991, the first example going to Reading Transport. The design was developed from the MCW Metrobus — DAF and Optare having bought the rights following its demise in 1989. The chassis was the DAF DB250, specially developed from the single-deck SB220 with a Metrobus-style driveline, with a new, low-emission 8.65 litre DAF engine and Metrobus-style rear suspension, while the Optare body is so far the only double-decker to use the Alusuisse bolted-aluminium structure. The first large order for the Spectra was for London Buses, 25 being delivered during 1992-3, numbered SP1-25 and registered F301-325 FYG. Twenty-four of these, SP1/3-25, were single-door, ordered as Routemaster replacements on route 3 (Oxford Circus-Crystal Palace) for London Central from January 1993, although they were used earlier on route 40 (Herne Hill-Poplar). Odd man out was dual-doored SP2 which went to Cricklewood, entering service there on routes 16/16A from October 1992, where it remained for about five months.

At privatisation, SP1/3-25 were with London Central, part of the Go-Ahead Group, while SP2 went to Stagecoach East London.

Left:
The impressive Optare Spectra, in this case London Central's SP11, on former Routemaster route 3 (Oxford Circus-Crystal Palace). It is seen shortly after leaving Oxford Circus in October 1993. *Kevin Lane*

Class LN

Chassis: Dennis Lance
Bodywork: Northern Counties
Numbers: LN1-31
Total: 31
Date new: 1993

Metroline was the recipient of the 31 members of the LN class, Dennis Lances fitted with 37-seat, dual-door Northern Counties Paladin bodies. LN1-31 were registered K301-31 YJA, entering service on two routes — the 113 (Edgware-Oxford Circus) from Cricklewood garage and the 302 (Mill Hill Broadway station-Notting Hill Gate) from Willesden garage from April 1993. All passed to the privatised Metroline in October 1994.

Left:
Metroline LN7 crossing Marylebone Road at Baker Street, working an Oxford Circus-bound 113 in December 1993. *Kevin Lane*

Below:
The LN class also worked the 302 from April 1993. LN19, in Mill Hill, heads for Notting Hill Gate in May 1994.
P. R. Wallis

Class VN

Class: VN
Chassis: Volvo B10B-58
Body: Northern Counties Paladin
Numbers: VN1-13 (total 13)
Dates new: 1993

These and the visually-similar LNs were the last standard-type full-size single-deckers delivered to London Buses Ltd, before the introduction of low-floor types. They typify the way things were going in London Transport, being based on a totally 'off-the-peg' type — though one not used elsewhere in dual-door form — and being supplied to work a specific London Transport contract, in this case to London General for the 88 (Oxford Circus-Clapham Common), which is run under the Clapham Omnibus brand name, and on which these 40-seat single-deckers were replacing double-deckers.

The Volvo B10B was at the time Volvo's standard rear-engined citybus chassis, which in the UK was introduced as the replacement for the Leyland Lynx, while the Northern Counties Paladin body was that builder's standard single-deck product. As well as being unique in London (though Trent runs similar, single-door, buses in Nottinghamshire and Derbyshire) they are also distinctive for carrying personalised number plates, with the initials of London General's managing director Keith Ludemann; they are K100, 2-6, 70, 8-13 KLL!

Above:
VN11 passes through Broad Sanctuary, alongside Westminster Abbey, when new in May 1993. *Stephen Morris*

Class LLW

Chassis: Dennis Lance SLF
Bodywork: Wright
Numbers: LLW1-38
Total: 38
Date new: 1994

Two classes of low-floor buses were introduced by London Buses, both in 1994. The first was the LLW class, Dennis Lance SLFs with Wright Pathfinder 34-seat dual-door bodywork, numbered LLW1-38 and registered ODZ 8901-24 and L25-38 WLH. Though not the very first low-floor, wheelchair-accessible buses to enter service in Britain, these vehicles with their step-free access to the forward part of the saloon, wheelchair ramps and space and kneeling suspension can be seen very much as the pioneers for a whole new concept in British buses They were distributed as follows: LLW1-10 went to London United for route 120 (Hounslow-Northolt) from January 1994, LLW11-24 began working on CentreWest route 222 (Hounslow-Uxbridge station) from March 1994, while Metroline took LLW25-38 for the 186 (Northwick Park Hospital-Edgware and Brent Cross) from June 1994. In each case Metrobuses were displaced. All vehicles passed to their respective privatised companies later in 1994.

Below:
West Drayton is the location of Centrewest LLW13, bearing the local 'Uxbridge Buses' identity, heading for home on a 222 working from Hounslow on 16 September 1994. Although Centrewest was sold to its management two weeks previously, LLW13 still carries its London Buses roundel. *P. R. Wallis*

Class LV

Chassis: Dennis Lance
Bodywork: Plaxton Verde
Numbers: LV1-12
Total: 12
Date new: 1994

The year 1994 saw the introduction of the LV class of Plaxton Verde-bodied Dennis Lance single-deckers. LV1-12 were allocated to Selkent's Catford garage for route 208 (Lewisham-Orpington), replacing Leyland Titans. The class was originally registered L201-12 YAG, although LV12 was subsequently re-registered WLT 461, formerly carried by Routemaster RM461 and StarRider SR1. When Selkent became part of the Stagecoach group in September 1994, all members of the class were included.

Below:
LV6 loading in Bromley High Street working on route 208 (Lewisham-Orpington), although only going as far as Petts Wood. The photograph was taken on 2 September 1994, just four days away from the sale of Selkent to Stagecoach. *Tony Wild*

Class SLW

Chassis: Scania N113CRL
Bodywork: Wright
Numbers: SLW1-30
Total: 30
Date new: 1994

The second class of low-floor buses, Scania N113CRLs with 37-seat Wright Pathfinder dual-door bodywork, has the distinction of providing the last buses to enter service with London Buses. SLW1-14, registered RDZ 1701-14, began on route 144 (Lower Edmonton-Muswell Hill) with Leaside, from September 1994, less than two weeks before Leaside became part of the Cowie Group. Of the rest of the batch, SLW15-30, only SLW15/17 had arrived at Upton Park before Stagecoach took over East London, the remainder going direct to the newly privatised company. They are used on route 101 (North Woolwich-Wanstead). Though other operators have taken buses very similar to the LLW class, these SLWs are unique to London.

Above:
Leaside Buses SLW2 at Turnpike Lane loading on a 144 journey to Edmonton Green station on 24 September 1994, five days before the sale to the Cowie Group. *P. R. Wallis*

Mini and Minibuses

With so many small buses running in London these days, it is surprising to remember that such operations commenced as long ago as 1972. There were, of course, small capacity buses around in pre-LPTB days, to be replaced by the C class of Leyland Cubs. With 20 seats, they were comparable in capacity with the later Ford Transits.

It was the GLC that initiated the idea of offering London Transport financial support to operate four routes with minibuses for a six-month experimental period. These routes, W9, C11, B1 and P4, have all expanded since their 1972 launch. Sixteen Ford Transits, numbered FS1-16 and registered MLK 701-16L, were used initially, carrying Strachan 16-seat bodies, while similar FS17 (MLK 717L) arrived early in 1973. Three further Ford Transits, FS18-20 (MLK 718-20L) were used to introduce a Dial-a-Bus scheme in Hampstead Garden Suburb in October 1974. This proved a success and another bus was ordered, which became FS21 (THM 721M). This was bodied by Dormobile as Strachan was, by then, no longer in business.

March 1977 saw a new FS route, local Potters Bar service PB1, by which time the original four FS routes had been converted to the larger BS class of Bristol. The Hampstead Garden Suburb service later became the H2, the original vehicles being replaced by Dormobile-bodied FS22-26 (CYT 22-26V) in 1979. These were in turn replaced by 20-seat Carlyle-bodied FS27-29 (C502-3 HOE) in 1985, which survived until the route was lost by LRT tender to R&I Tours in June 1989. (R&I Tours took over another former FS route, the C11, in 1990.) The last survivor, and the only one to pass to a privatised company, was Westlink's FS29.

The Potters Bar local route PB1 later required slightly larger vehicles. These materialised as a pair of Rootes-bodied Dodge 50s, arriving in December 1982 as 20-seaters, but entering service in the following March after being down-seated to 19. They were numbered A1 and A2 with the registrations NYN 1/2Y. The PB1 was lost to North Mymms Coaches in June 1986, when they were sent south to Orpington for the start of the Roundabout services in the August.

1986 saw the introduction of another minibus class, the OV, Optare CityPacers, whose futuristic styling and high driving position strove to leave the old bread-van image behind. The first five, OV1-5, went to Orpington to work alongside RH class Ivecos on Roundabout routes. They wore a maroon and grey livery and were named after winds. Later in the year, in October, OV6-24 began tourist-oriented route C1 between Westminster and Kensington. Dual-purpose seating and stereo radios were fitted. In the evenings, they were used on experimental routes C20/21 between Waterloo and Victoria via the West End.

Further vehicles, OV25-49, were leased by LRT to London Country (North West) for tendered route C2 from March 1987, passing with the route to London Buses in June 1988. The last three, OV50-53, were fitted with wheelchair lifts for Carelink duties from March 1988. These vehicles were used until January

Below:
Ford Transit FS20 at Golders Green in May 1977, working the Hampstead Garden Suburb service, H2. *Tony Wild*

1993 when the service was relaunched as Stationlink and new Mercedes were put into service by the new operator, Kensington independent Frank E. Thorpe, who had used the OVs since taking over the service in the previous October.

The Iveco Daily has become a familiar sight on the streets of Britain and although London Buses only took a total of 42, they have constituted three classes. The first was the RH class, 24 Iveco Daily 49.10s with Robin Hood 21-seater bodywork. Most of these were allocated to Orpington for Roundabout duties from the summer of 1986, although RH14/9, 20/22 were loaned to Eastbourne Buses, receiving blue and cream livery, from October until the end of the year. RH19/22 later were used by London Coaches, helping out on Chelsea Harbour Hoppa route C3 from its introduction in April 1987 until they moved on to Orpington late in 1989. From January 1988, the Bexleybus scheme also used members of the RH class.

The next class of Ivecos were Reeve Burgess-bodied FR1-8, entering service on local Hounslow routes H24/25 from January 1991. They have seating for 20, although they are fitted with rear doors for wheelchair access. With two wheelchairs on board, seating is reduced by four. The buses were finished in white and green Hounslow Hoppa livery and were in fact bought by the London Borough of Hounslow and operated on its behalf by London United from Hounslow garage.

The final Ivecos were the FM class, Marshall 23-seat bodywork being fitted. FM1-10 replaced earlier Ivecos of the RH class on Roundabout routes from May 1993.

The integral MCW Metrorider, available from 1986, was an early success and sold well to many urban operators, its styling showing some influence of Optare CityPacer. The first for London Buses were with Westlink for use on three routes of the Kingston network, K1/2/3 introduced in June 1987. These were Cummins-engined MR1-22 (D461-82 PON). The class soon became widespread throughout much of London, finding use on local schemes such as Harrow and Bexleyheath. A longer version, the MRL, was also supplied, with later vehicles being built by Optare, who bought the design from MCW in 1989. The class was delivered until 1993, the last going to London Central. To summarise, the class consisted of MR1-64/93-105/134 and MRL65-92/106-133/135-241. MR134 was formerly an MCW demonstrator, while a non-operative MRL was specially built by Optare for the London Transport Museum in 1993. It is sectioned and can be 'driven' using a simulator. MR93-98 entered service as SG1-6 and ran as such for a short period during August 1988, being used on routes G1/2 in Tooting.

In April 1987 London Coaches began operation of the Chelsea Harbour Hoppa route C3 between Earls Court and Chelsea Harbour, the initial service using a pair of Carlyle-bodied Freight Rover Sherpas, SC1/2 (D585 OOV and D974 PJW), and two Ivecos, RH19/22. SC1 later became a trainer, SC2 being returned to Carlyle (as dealer) in 1989, the C3 being subsequently operated by several

types including OV, SR and MRL classes. Two Sherpas used to form a new class were Dormobile-bodied SD1/2 (D811 KWT and D212 GLJ), new to West Riding and Shamrock & Rambler respectively. They were used from 1990 on a contract for the Department of Health, operating from Clapton.

The year 1988 saw the introduction of the first of many Mercedes-based vehicles to operate for London Buses. Optare StarRiders, based on the MB811 chassis were put into service during 1988-89 forming the SR class. The first four went to Selkent in July 1988, with later deliveries including Harrow, Bexleyheath and Peckham. A total of 123 entered service, although SR10 was withdrawn following fire damage in 1990.

Reeve Burgess-bodied MB709Ds with rear wheelchair lifts were specified for the Southall Shuttle, route E5, from November 1989, becoming MT1-5, while two further members of the class, MT7/8, arrived in August 1990. MT6 was a trainer/private hire vehicle at Catford and, unusually, featured dual control. MTL1-5 were a longer

Opposite top:
In lieu of an A class Dodge in Potters Bar, we have A2 pulling out of Kingston bus station in July 1987. It had been in use for driver training prior to the introduction of minibuses by Westlink during the previous month. *Kevin Lane*

Opposite bottom:
The last three OV class Optare CityPacers, OV50-52, were suitably equipped for the Carelink service between the major London railway termini, beginning and ending at Waterloo. The service was contracted to London General, in whose care OV52 is seen at Euston station in September 1989. *Kevin Lane*

Above:
Robin Hood-bodied Iveco Daily 49-10 RH23, named *Hawk*, seen negotiating Orpington War Memorial on Roundabout route R1 in August 1986, a couple of months after entry into service. This was one of the class that later donned Bexleybus colours. *Kevin Lane*

Top:
FR8 in Hounslow Hoppa white livery, picking up in Feltham High Street in August 1991. *R. J. Waterhouse*

Above:
The FM class entered service at Orpington from April 1993, replacing RH class Ivecos. Here FM1 pauses in the rain while working on route R8 in the following December. *P. R. Wallis*

Top Right:
A few Metroriders also saw operation in Bexleybus blue and cream, including MR55 (Bexleybus 31) in Bexleyheath in January 1988 at the start of the scheme. *Kevin Lane*

Right:
SD1, one of the two Sherpas employed on Department of Health contract services, is caught in traffic at Waterloo in August 1990. *Kevin Lane*

B12 ERITH
TSB
ALAN'S
Bexleybus
hoppa
MCW
E631 KYW

PRIVATE SERVICE
LONDON FOREST
LONDON FOREST
D811 KWT
F397 JMV

Top:
The clean lines of the Optare StarRider are seen to good effect in this 1991 view of SR90 working for Metroline at Brent Cross on route 143. *Kevin Lane*

Above:
MA101 on Gold Arrow route 28 at Golders Green in July 1991. This was one of seven (MA101-107) fitted with dual-purpose seating for private hire work if required. MA101 was originally registered F701 XMS, but received that from RM31 in May 1989. *Kevin Lane*

Above:
The red livery is relieved by a broad white band on the MT class used on the E5, Southall Shuttle. MT1 is seen in Dormer's Wells Lane in December 1988. *R. J. Waterhouse*

Below:
MC4 in Crown Lane, Bromley Common, in July 1991, working on Roundabout route R1. *Tony Wild*

version of the MT, with increased seating and with no facility for wheelchairs. MT6 later became MTL6.

The largest class of Mercedes was the 134-strong MA class, featuring Alexander bodywork. The first vehicles were involved in the launch of the Uxbridge area U4 service in February 1989, although this was eclipsed by the conversion of Routemaster routes 28 and 31 to the type under the Gold Arrow banner in the March and April. Further MAs went to Uxbridge for new U-line services in the May. Later deliveries went to Putney and Victoria. The 28 and 31 were converted to DW class Dennis Darts during early 1991.

A Carlyle-bodied Mercedes 811D was a demonstrator at Catford from July 1989. Registered F430 BOP, it was taken into stock in April 1990, becoming MC1. The class was completed by the arrival of MC2-5 (H882-5 LOX), set to work on Roundabout route R3 at Orpington.

The first Wright-bodied Mercedes of the MW class, MW1-16, appeared at Catford in December 1989, operating on several routes alongside StarRiders. MW18-37 went for service with London Northern at Potters Bar. MW17 has a revised front end, a 'fast front' style which Wright developed for Ulsterbus.

Wright bodywork was also fitted to the RW class of Renaults delivered during 1990. All 90 went to CentreWest, RW1-14 allowing the conversion of the 282 from Metrobus, while the rest were introduced onto Ealing area E routes. RW14 was burnt out and withdrawn in 1994.

Specialist vehicles to enter the fleet in 1989-90 were seven CVE/Omni 20-seat minibuses. CV1-3 were owned by the London Borough of Hounslow and operated by Westlink on LRT tendered route H20, while CV4 was for the Carelink service. Up to two wheelchairs could be accommodated, which reduced the seating

Above:
Standing outside Northwood Hills Metropolitan Line station is RW5 working a 282 towards Ealing Hospital in June 1990. *Kevin Lane*

Below:
CV3 at Hounslow Central on its customary route, the H20, on a dreary December morning in 1990. *Kevin Lane*

Top right:
RB4 leads a Kentish Bus Olympian on route 22A and an RM on a 38 along Mare Street, Hackney, in March 1991. RB4 was withdrawn in 1994 and later became Yorkshire Traction 374. *Kevin Lane*

Below right:
London United's DT21 is caught in Hounslow working on the H98 as Leyland National LS419 overtakes on an H22. Both are bound for Hounslow bus station in December 1990. *Kevin Lane*

NORTH WOOLWICH FERRY
Stratford Hackney
276
hoppa
EAST LONDON
Turbo
G874 WML
Kentis
38

H22
HOUNSLOW
CROWN YARD
BYW 419V
H98
Harrier
LONDON UNITED
Dart
G521 VYE

by seven. CV5-7 were also operated by Westlink, this time at Richmond on routes R61/62. They carried the unusual registrations of A2-4 LBR, requested by the London Borough of Richmond.

Other Renaults were the short-lived Reeve Burgess-bodied RB class, RB1-35. The first 25 were for midibus conversions in the East End in February 1990, while a second batch of eight followed in the October. All went to Bow garage (and later to Stratford outstation) for routes S2, 100, 241, 276 and 278. RB34/5 had Plaxton bodies and were loaned by Renault in 1992, the former going to the East End with others, the latter heading west to Uxbridge.

The mini and midibus were traditionally front-engined

Above:
Wright-bodied Dennis Dart DWL1 carrying an all-over livery for Kingston University, mainly white with blue flashes. It is seen in Surbiton working a contract for the university in December 1993. Metrorider MR134 wore a similar livery at this time. *Kevin Lane*

Below:
DRL33 turns into Pancras Road, King's Cross, in June 1994 working between Farringdon Street and Kensal Rise station, a route formerly operated by StarRiders, and Titans before that. *Kevin Lane*

Right:
The DNL class of Dennis Darts carry Northern Counties Paladin bodywork. Most are branded for the C2 'Camden Link' service operated by London Northern; here DNL109 is seen in Regent Street in August 1994. *P. R. Wallis*

van-based vehicles, but this was to change with the introduction of the rear-engined Dennis Dart, which entered service in some numbers and varieties, six makers of bodywork having appeared by 1994. First off were the DT class, totalling 168 vehicles and delivered in 1990-91. DT1-27 were bodied by Duple and went to Fulwell and Hounslow with London United, while the rest received Carlyle bodies to the same design and were dispatched to Orpington, Bromley, Thornton Heath, Willesden, Edgware, North Wembley and Stamford Brook. The second Dart variant arrived at the end of 1990 in the shape of the Wright-bodied DW class, whose twin windscreen gave the vehicle a look of the RF. DW1-14 went to CentreWest for the 297, replacing Metrobuses, while a longer version, the DWL, was employed by Westlink for its 371, numbered DWL1-14. Further Wright-bodied Darts went far and wide, including Westbourne Park (where DW15-43 replaced MAs on Gold Arrow duties), Wood Green, Catford and Sutton. A final batch of DWLs, 15-26, went to East London.

The Dennis Dart was rapidly becoming another standard London type. The largest variant entered service between 1991 and 1994 as the Plaxton Pointer-bodied DR/DRL classes, which totalled 324 vehicles: DR1-153 and DRL1-171. They became a common sight in many parts of the capital, with the largest concentrations being found with London United and London General.

The last two classes of Dart to enter service with London Buses were quite small and were for specific routes. The DNL class were 34-seat Northern Counties Paladin-bodied Darts, bought in order to convert route C2 (Oxford Circus-Parliament Hill Fields) from SR operation. Numbered DNL101-110/112-120 they were branded as the 'Camden Link' (except 118/119) and worked from Holloway garage.

Also in 1994 came DEL1-11, East Lancs EL2000-bodied Darts for the 484 at Camberwell. The Dart continues to enter service with the privatised companies; indeed, the first buses to be ordered by the new regimes were 9.8m Plaxton-bodied Darts for Metroline, classified EDR.

By the time that the various London bus fleets passed into private ownership, several minibus classes had disappeared. Only one Ford Transit, FS29, remained, as did only three RH class Ivecos, while both A class Dodges had gone, along with all of the OV and RB classes. The latter were all acquired by the Yorkshire Traction Group, subsequently operating for RoadCar, Lincoln City, Strathtay and Yorkshire Traction itself. A noteworthy addition to the London Transport Museum collection is Optare CityPacer OV2. To summarise the position at privatisation — CentreWest has MA, MT, MTL, MW, DW and RW classes; East London: MR, MRL, SR, DW, DWL, DRL; Leaside: MR, SR, DRL; London Central: MR, MRL, SR, MTL, DRL, DEL; London General: SC (driver trainer), MA, MRL, MT, DR, DRL, DW; London Northern: MRL, MW, SR, DRL, DNL; London United: MRL, DT, DR, DRL, FR; Metroline: MR, SR, DT, DR; Selkent: RH, MR, MRL, MA, MW, MT, MTL, MC, DW, FM, DT; South London: MR, MRL, SR, DT, DR, DRL; Westlink: FS, MR, MRL, DWL, CV.

LT and BEA

At the end of the war there was a tremendous increase in commercial air travel. With land communications across Europe severely disrupted, but plenty of military airfields, aircraft became increasingly important in postwar transport.

British European Airways Division (BEA) was formed in February 1946. Initially operating from Northolt, its first flight from Heathrow took place in April 1950. Unlike BOAC, which chose to operate its own coaches from its Victoria terminal, BEA contracted its services out to the LPTB which maintained and operated the coaches, Commer Commandos and Bedford OBs, from Gillingham Street garage. In May 1948, a new terminal was opened in Kensington in order to cope with the increase in traffic, while the contractor became the LTE, as successor to the LPTB.

The backbone of the early coach fleet were Commer Commandos with Park Royal bodies, generally 18 or 20-seaters, but with substantial luggage space, similar in layout to the inter-station Leyland Cubs. As time went on, it became clear that these vehicles would need to be replaced by something larger. The replacements materialised as the well-known Park Royal-bodied AEC Regal IVs; with 37 seats as well as extra luggage accommodation they were more than up to the job. They were built in two batches — MLL713-729 in 1952, with MLL 730-762 and NLP 636-650 following in 1953 — a total of 65 vehicles. The Park Royal bodies were designed by London Transport and featured a flat roofline within a 1½-deck layout. They were fitted with Green Line type seats and received the classification of 4RF4 from London Transport. During the delivery of these vehicles, a number of the 10T10 class AEC Regals were loaned by London Transport to assist the Commers.

The 4RF4s maintained the service throughout the 1950s, also being used to and from Gatwick from 1958, those vehicles being allocated to Reigate garage. Both the terminal point and the garage used by the 4RF4s changed during this period. A temporary terminal at Waterloo, opened in 1953 to replace Kensington, was itself superseded by permanent premises at Cromwell Curve as the West London Air Terminal in 1957. The BEA fleet was subsequently moved to the garage at Shepherds Bush, and again, in 1960, to the old trolleybus depot at Hammersmith.

In the early 1960s consideration was given to the use of double-deckers on the Heathrow run. To this end, BEA took delivery of 220 CXK, an AEC Regent V with Park Royal H37/18F bodywork, in December 1961, to test its suitability. Further trials were carried out between June 1964 and November 1966 using RMF1254 (254 CLT), the forward-entrance Routemaster on loan from London Transport. In order to carry as many passengers as possible, the extra luggage space was provided by a separate two-wheeled trailer. This combination proved to be successful and 65 forward-entrance Routemasters with 88 trailers were duly ordered to replace the Regals. Similar ideas of double-decking were taking place with BOAC, which had received a Leyland Atlantean (VFR 373) on loan from Standerwick in 1965. The type was subsequently ordered for use on the Victoria-Heathrow service, although with an on-board luggage area rather than a separate trailer. In common with the 4RF4s before them, the Routemasters were delivered in two batches: KGJ 601-625D came towards the end of 1966, while NMY 626-665E arrived early in 1967. They were numbered BEA1-65 by London Transport and all carried Park Royal H32/24F bodywork. The 4RF4s were duly withdrawn, most being resold by Bird's Commercial Motors, Stratford-upon-Avon, mostly ending up in non-PSV use. Three were sold directly to London Transport in 1967 for use as mobile uniform stores, while several have passed into preservation.

Other new coaches delivered around this time were eight Willowbrook-bodied AEC Reliances, used on a new Executive Express service for passengers on UK internal flights. These were registered KHM 1-8D and were new in July 1966. They were

given the fleet numbers EC1-8 by London Transport. The service had actually started in July 1965, using hired Green Line RF290-7, which were returned to London Transport after a year. In 1966 there was yet another change in the allocation of BEA vehicles, from Hammersmith to the old Chiswick Tram depot.

From 1 April 1974 BEA became the European Division of British Airways, with all of the Routemasters and the EC class AEC Reliances passing to the new owners. The Executive Express service had ceased back in March 1973, the vehicles being used in normal service alongside the Routemasters. A decline in the West London Air Terminal to Heathrow service was setting in. The Reliances were soon sold and reductions in the service saw the gradual withdrawal of the Routemasters also. The Piccadilly Line extension to Heathrow Central, opened in December 1977, effectively sealed the fate of the coach service, which finally came to an end in March 1979. The Routemasters were disposed of to London Transport for staff and driver training duties in three batches in 1975/76/79 (those from the 1975 batch were initially used, following suitable modifications, on route 175, during 1975/76). From August 1978 the survivors had been operating from Stonebridge garage.

Opposite:
BEA '4RF4', MLL 714 — the second to be delivered in June 1952 — stands at Heathrow, probably in the early 1960s. This particular vehicle was numbered 1071, although this was only carried on a plate on the dashboard. Sold in 1967, 1071 along with 1087 (MLL 728) became mobile showrooms for Yardley International in Milan and Frankfurt respectively. Still together, the pair ended up as catering buses in the film industry, both going for scrap in 1971. *A. B. Cross*

Below:
Routemaster 8217 of the 1966 delivery in original condition. The livery was blue and white, with black mudguards and band between the decks. From 1969 a red and white livery was introduced, while some, but not all, received the blue and white British Airways colours following its inception in 1974. No 8217, by then numbered C217, passed to London Transport in June 1979, part of the last batch to do so, to become RMA36. *V. C. Jones/IAL*

LT Coaching

London Transport withdrew its private hire fleet in 1963, while the Green Line operations passed to London Country in 1970, thus allowing LT to concentrate on bus operation. Of course, private hire work was still undertaken, but using ordinary vehicles; the sight of RTs or Routemasters at seaside resorts on the south and east coasts was quite usual. In 1984 the Tours & Charter Division of London Regional Transport decided to evaluate a coach. A new era began with the arrival of B593 XNO, a DAF coach with Berkhof Esprite bodywork on lease from Ensignbus, in a white livery with rainbow stripes.

The Tours & Charters Division, a cumbersome if accurate title, was relaunched as London Coaches in 1986, immediately offering a high profile. Although its main interest was sightseeing work, its coaching activities took off with the development of a quality London-Birmingham service, jointly operated with West Midlands PTE. It took to the road in March 1986 branded as 'London Liner', the intention being to compete with the National Express Rapide services, offering a steward service, free hot drinks, videos, telephone, a toilet and so on. Initially, London Coaches used a pair of Duple Caribbean II-bodied DAFs, while West Midlands PTE ran Bova Futuras. Later both operators replaced their vehicles with double-deck MCW Metroliners. Another initiative was a second joint service, to Eastbourne. London Coaches contributed a pair of East Lancs-bodied Leyland Olympians, similar to those used by the other partner, Eastbourne Buses. Sadly, neither service lived up to expectations and London Coaches withdrew within a year.

The coach fleet grew steadily, standardising on the DAF/Van Hool combination which became the DV class. Operations were transferred from Battersea to Wandsworth in April 1988, the same month in which the workings of Bexleyheath Transport were acquired. Furthermore, the commuter operations of Redwing Coaches were gained in March 1990. This network of commuter services has grown into what is currently the North Kent Express operations. London Coaches was the first of the London Bus units to be privatised, in May 1992.

In the meantime, some of the other London Bus units began operating coaches for private hire and contract duties. A variety of new and used vehicles were allocated, including Leyland Leopards and Tigers, DAFs and Volvos. A notable acquisition was that of E469 YWJ, a Neoplan Skyliner double-decker, which was bought by London Northern in 1991, receiving the classification SKY1. Coach numbering has followed a self-explanatory system: D for DAF, L for Leyland Leopard, T for Leyland Tiger, V for Volvo, and so on. Thus, DD is DAF/Duple and TPL is Leyland Tiger/Plaxton for example. Westlink's Volvo/Duple is, perhaps understandably, numbered VT1. At the privatisation of London

Left:
The coach that started it all: DAF/Berkhof B593 XNO is pictured outside 55 Broadway before it was officially handed over by DAF Bus and Ensign to London Transport in September 1984. It was numbered TC1 in 1985 and renumbered DB1 in 1986. On the expiry of its lease in 1990, it passed to CharterCoach, Harwich. *G. R. Mills*

Below:
Metroliner ML1 squeezing out of Battersea garage to take up service to Birmingham, from Wilton Road coach station. Battersea garage had been closed in November 1985, but was later reopened to house the coaching fleet, together with the RLST fleet. These were transferred to the current premises at Wandsworth in April 1988. With the withdrawal of the Birmingham service from March 1987, the Metroliners were disposed of, ML1/2/4 passing to Central Coachways, Birmingham, while ML3 went to Busways, Newcastle. *L. J. Long*

Opposite top:
One of the two East Lancs-bodied Leyland Olympians used on the Eastbourne service, LC1 is seen on layover at the seaside town in 1986. After the withdrawal of the Eastbourne service in October 1987, the two coaches were used for private hire duties before being sold to Southampton. *Kevin Lane Collection*

Opposite centre left:
The standard London Coaches combination was DAF/Van Hool; DV2 was an early example and is seen at Woburn Abbey when new in 1987. DV2 passed to the privatised London Coaches in 1994. *Kevin Lane*

Buses in 1994, the coach distribution was as follows: Selkent: DD35/36, DP1, DV36-39/67; East London: TPL6/7, VP2; Leaside: LP5/6; Metroline: LD5; London Northern: SKY1, VP1; Westlink: VT1.

Bottom:
The impressive London Northen Neoplan Skyliner, SKY1. Allocated to Holloway, it is seen at the Cambridge City FC coach park in july 1991. *G. R. Mills*

Below right:
Another London Northern Vehicle is Volvo B10M/Plaxton VP1, seen at Butlins, Bognor Regis in May 1994. It was previously with Park, Hamilton, as G91 RGG in 1993, but received the registration NDZ 7936 from Mercedes MW36. *Kevin Lane*

LRT Tendering

One of the most significant events in the history of London bus operation is route tendering. Section 6 of the 1984 London Regional Transport Act required the contracting out of certain services as appropriate. While this included such activities as the catering at 55 Broadway, not likely to set the bus enthusiast's pulse racing, putting out bus services to competitive tender has certainly added considerable interest, not to mention colour, to the London bus scene.

The broad aim of LRT was to reduce the amount of subsidy paid to London Buses by being more cost effective. This was to be achieved by allowing independent operators, as well as London Buses Ltd, to bid to operate those services put out to tender by LRT. Successful operators must work within LRT guidelines with regards to fares, acceptance of travelcards, types of vehicles employed and so on, with LRT providing publicity. Put simply, the contract was arranged whereby LRT pays the operator the cost of running the service, while retaining the fares collected.

The first package of routes to be put out to tender commenced operation in July/August 1985, the successful bidders being London Buses (routes 84A, 152, 215, 228, 258 and H2), Len Wright Travel trading as London Buslines (route 81), Crystals of Orpington (route 146), Eastern National (routes 193 and W9) and London Country (routes 313 and P4). These routes, together with the second batch awarded in December 1985 for

Above:
Among the first batch of tenders was route 146 (Bromley North-Downe), previously worked by LS class Leyland Nationals from Bromley garage. Crystals of Orpington took over operations in August 1985, successfully retaining the tender in 1988, but lost it to Metrobus, Orpington, in August 1991. Crystals HTI-Maxeta-bodied Leyland Cub C924 DKR leaves Bromley for Downe in August 1986, a year into the contract. Up until April 1978 one could have travelled to Downe in an RT or RM! *Kevin Lane*

Below:
The first Jonckheere bus bodies in the UK appeared on five Scania K92s with Scancoaches, Harlesden, when they commenced operation of the 283 from May 1986. C351 SVV is seen leaving Shepherds Bush (or Schepherds Bush as the blind has it) for Hammersmith hospital in June 1986. *Kevin Lane*

Right:
Many elderly vehicles found their way into LRT service in the early years of the tendering system; this London Country (South West) — later London & Country — Alexander-bodied Leyland Atlantean came from Greater Glasgow PTE and was new in 1974. It is waiting in Epsom to return to Hackbridge on a route 293 journey, operated from July 1986, in May 1987.
Kevin Lane Collection

Below:
The Bexleybus scheme, as well as having new Leyland Olympians, also boasted the dubious delights of former London DMSs that had operated for some time with Western SMT and Clydeside Scottish. One of these, formerly DMS1679 but now Bexleybus 86, works route 96 through Bexleyheath in February 1988. The 96 passed to Kentish Bus in January 1991. *Kevin Lane*

commencement in March 1986, were all deliberately spread throughout the Outer London area and all were ripe for cost-cutting.

Subsequent tendering has taken some interesting turns. The third round took a different approach in that a whole group of routes in one area, in this case Orpington, were put out at once. The result was that London Buses, which won the contract to operate a network of minibus routes within the scheme, set up a subsidiary, Orpington Buses Ltd, trading as Roundabout. London Buses subsequently set up similar types of operations in Bexleyheath, Harrow, Kingston and Sutton, in the cases of the first two introducing new colour schemes. Another notable subsidiary was Stanwell Buses, trading as Westlink. This was originally set up in 1986 in order to operate services won by tender from Surrey County Council, although LRT tendered services were also bid for and won. Westlink was privatised in January 1994 ahead of the other bus operating units.

Above:
Boro'line Maidstone won its first LRT tenders in January 1988, including the 132 and 228 in southeast London. Optare-bodied Leyland Olympians were put into service, as illustrated here by 751. The vehicle is pulling in behind a hired Kingston upon Hull Leyland Atlantean on route 228 at Eltham station shortly after the start of the contracts. Sadly Boro'line went into receivership in February 1992, its London commitments passing to Kentish Bus. *Kevin Lane*

Below:
A short-lived operator of LRT contracts was Frontrunner South East, which was actually part of East Midland, later owned by Stagecoach, and maintained the services from Mansfield. Four routes were operated in east London, tendered routes 248, 252 and 347 together with schooldays route 550. Operations lasted from September 1988 (initially sub-contracted to Grey-Green although using East Midland vehicles) until wound up the following June, when Ensign took over the contracts. A pair of former Greater Manchester Leyland Atlanteans pass in Hornchurch on 252 workings during the first month of Frontrunner South East operations. *Kevin Lane*

Great interest was shown when the first central London route was won by a non-London Buses operator. From November 1988, route 24 (Hampstead Heath-Pimlico) was operated by Grey-Green using a fleet of Volvo Citybuses. Other operators followed — Kentish Bus, London & Country and BTS of Borehamwood all penetrating the Central Area. Notable was the use of Routemasters by Kentish Bus on route 19 and BTS on route 13, refurbished RMLs leased from LRT.

In the early days, the independent operators used a wide variety of vehicles on their tendered services — often elderly, secondhand machines. Ex-London DMSs could often be encountered, together with Leyland Atlanteans, Bristol VRTs, Leyland Nationals and the odd coach or two. The first operator to buy new buses was Scancoaches, which bought five 12m Jonckheere-bodied Scania K92s for route 283, later lost to London Buses. The midibus has become an increasing feature of the tendered scene, while both London Buses and the independents have invested in new full-sized rolling stock in recent years. This has brought a considerable variety of buses into London service. The independents usually have their own vehicle policies, while the various London Buses companies have become increasingly autonomous, allowing them to buy whatever buses they need for a specific contract. In any case, if new buses are required for a new service at a particular date, then vehicles are sometimes needed at short notice and they have to take what is available. The age of these buses has come down in any case, as a ruling was made that vehicles used on new LRT tenders should be no more than seven years old, other than where Routemasters are specified.

The tendering procedure has continued apace through privatisation. By mid-1994 half of the capital's bus services were operated under tender, with half of these in the hands of London Buses subsidiaries, and the latest development is that operators have to take the revenue risk on new tenders, bidding on the basis of minimum subsidy rather than minimum cost.

Above:
Grey-Green won the tender from London Buses for route 125 (North Finchley-Winchmore Hill) in November 1987. The route usually saw ex-Greater Manchester Daimler Fleetlines in service. Here, however, is seen an unusual vehicle in March 1988 — an Alexander-bodied Scania of A1 of Ardrossan, in use as a Scania demonstrator. The location is Southgate. *Kevin Lane*

Below:
R&I Tours, well known for its Dennis Darts introduced onto the C11/12 routes in July 1990, had several LRT contracts before that, including local Harrow route H17 operated between September 1989 and February 1991 when Sovereign Bus and Coach took over. Included in the fleet were four Lex Maxeta-bodied Bedford YMQSs that were new to South Wales Transport in 1982, an example of which is LCY 299X seen in Harrow in September 1990. *Kevin Lane*

Above:
London Suburban Buses, the subsidiary of Liverpool-based GEMSAM Holdings, won several tenders in 1993, including route 4 (Waterloo-Archway). Ex-London Leyland Titans were used initially, although other types such as C376 CAS, a 1986 Alexander RL-bodied Leyland Olympian, new to Highland, about to cross Waterloo Bridge in May 1994, have appeared. *Kevin Lane*

Below:
London Buses bought small batches of vehicles for specific tenders, a far cry from the 1950s, when it would have had to have been either an RT or an RF! On other occasions, it has turned towards the secondhand market. The Harrow network included both leased and secondhand double-deckers, the latter consisting of former West Midlands Travel Volvo Ailsas, introduced from November 1987. V50 approaches Golders Green station in the pouring rain, working in from Pinner on a 183 in 1988. As was usual with contracts operated by London Buses, no LRT board is carried. *Kevin Lane*

Hired Buses, Demonstrators and Others

Almost all bus operators, however large or well organised, have had to bring in extra vehicles for one reason or another in order to maintain services. Such periods are always fascinating for the enthusiast and London Transport has proved no exception. Throughout its history, many unfamiliar vehicles have found themselves pressed into traffic.

The first such occasion occurred early in World War 2. The Blitz on London began in August 1940 with transport becoming an immediate target, so much so that in the October an appeal was made by London Transport to operators in the provinces to send surplus vehicles. Not only were buses being damaged by enemy action, but the disruption of train, tram and trolleybus services necessitated the running of emergency buses, all putting a strain on the existing fleet.

Operators outside London certainly rose to the occasion, with a total of 390 double-deckers, 85 single-deckers and coaches and 18 trolleybuses being loaned over a period of a year or so. They came from all over the country, mainly company and municipal, although several independents chipped in with a few vehicles. Manchester Corporation supplied the most buses, 92 double-deckers mainly Crossleys, with

Glasgow coming second, contributing 39 Albions and Leyland TD1 Titans. Many others loaned vehicles, including Birmingham (30), Bolton (25), Exeter (3), Hants & Dorset (8), Leeds (24), North Western (16), Sheffield (12) and Youngs, Paisley (3). The actual rolling stock showed plenty of variety, types including reasonably modern Leyland TD Titans, AEC Regents, Daimlers and Dennises, few older than 1930. However, older, more exotic fare could be found — such as the 14 Bristol Bs of 1929 supplied by United Automobile, the three 1928

Previous page top:
On 1 July 1933, the LPTB took over the Gravesend and Dartford area operations of Maidstone & District. Amongst the vehicles acquired were 34 Leyland TD1 double-deckers, dating from 1928-31, which duly became TD133-166 with the Board. Two of these, TD156/60, passed to Youngs Motor Services, Paisley, in 1940, with the latter, Short-bodied TD160, returning on hire between October 1940 and March 1941. It is seen here working on route 15 from Upton Park garage. Youngs supplied two other London Leyland TD1s: former TD6, acquired from Nelson Omnibus Co, London E4, and TD20, ex-United Omnibus Co, London SW9. *V. C. Jones Collection/IAL*

Previous page bottom:
The hiring of coaches during the 1947-49 period brought much vehicular variety to London's bus scene. Rather more modern than many of the coaches pressed into service is this Grey-Green Bedford OB waiting at Victoria station to work a 76 to Edmonton. More usual fare on the 76 is London Transport's G7, parked a little way behind, but going only as far as Tottenham. *J. F. Higham*

Above:
Leeds Corporation hired AEC Regents to London Transport at Bromley garage between November 1949 and July 1950. Leeds 186 is working on a 61 journey between Well Hall station and Bromley garage. *V. C. Jones/IAL*

Below:
Maidstone Corporation loaned three new Brush-bodied Daimler CVG6s to London Transport during 1949-50. They were all operated from Sutton garage, from where 82 was working on route 93 between Putney Bridge and Morden at South Wimbledon in August 1950 when this photograph was taken. *V. C. Jones/IAL*

Right:
Eastern National lowbridge Brush-bodied Guy Arab II 3879 during its period on hire to London Transport between September and December 1951. It stands in Clarence Road, Grays, on route 31 to Tilbury Town station, which subsequently became, with alterations, routes 371/371A. *V. C. Jones/IAL*

ADC single-deckers, part of Eastern Counties loan, and the only Guys, five six-wheel Grose-bodied FCXs from Northampton. Interestingly, the three Leyland TD1 Titans supplied by Youngs of Paisley had been sold by London Transport earlier in the year!

At first, buses were sent wherever they were needed the most, regardless of type. However, it soon became the policy to allocate similar types together, including the transfer of all single-deckers to the Country Area. The buses spent varying lengths of time in the capital, with some staying only a month or two before returning home. Almost all had moved on by the end of 1941, the last leaving in September 1942, although these were some of the Bournemouth trolleybuses, sent north to Newcastle.

By the end of 1941 the Luftwaffe was concentrating its attacks elsewhere in Britain and it was the turn of London Transport to loan vehicles out. A total of 291 STs spent a varying amount of time with 47 provincial operators, the first leaving in November 1941, the last not returning until as late as 1948. Eight C class Cubs were also out on loan during the period 1942-45.

London Transport was soon to find itself in difficulties again. There was a postwar boom in travel, coming at a time when many buses were off the road because of a chronic lack of spares. Coupled with the shortage of new buses — of 4,000 new RTs on order at the end of 1947, only 182 had actually been delivered — a second period of mass hiring of buses took place. This time the immediate solution was nearer to home. Between 1947 and 1949 a considerable number of coaches, over 500, were hired for relief duties between Mondays to Fridays, London Transport conductors accompanying drivers supplied with the coaches. As can be imagined, all sorts of vehicles, provided that they were presentable and roadworthy, were pressed into service, representing most makes around at the time — so much for postwar standardisation! Lucky was the enthusiast with a camera (and film to put in it!).

In 1948 came nationalisation and the setting up of the LTE under the control of the British Transport Commission. It was now possible to divert new buses from other members of the group to ease the shortage in London. Some 170 ECW-bodied Bristol K types were delivered straight to London from the bodybuilder for service, moving on to their intended owners during 1949-50. These were loaned by Brighton, Hove & District (7), Caledonian (2), Crosville (30), Eastern Counties (38), Eastern National (12), Hants & Dorset (19), Southern National (8), Southern Vectis (2), United (17), United Counties (8), Westcliff-on-Sea (3) and Western National (24). Further to the Bristols were a trio of Brush-bodied Daimler CVG6s diverted from Maidstone Corporation, and a number of prewar AEC Regents loaned by Leeds. As 1950 progressed, new vehicles were arriving in quantity, the last loaned buses going home in the September.

The next short period of vehicles being loaned occurred late in 1951. With London Transport now nationalised, some attempts were made to rationalise services with its nationalised neighbours. At the end of September 1951, the services of Eastern National in the Tilbury and Grays area were transferred to London Transport. Although the garage in Argent Street, Grays, and its staff came to London Transport, the buses did not. However, they stayed, on loan, until the end of the year. Twenty-eight vehicles were involved: five Dennis Lancets dating from 1933-4, 10 utility Brush-bodied Guy Arabs, a pair of Beadle-bodied Bedford OBs and a collection of 11 single-deck Bristols. All of these received gold London Transport fleetnames, although not all actually appeared in service, only the Guys and Bristols being used at all extensively. These loaned vehicles ran alongside STLs until returned to Eastern National, while RTs arrived for full integration of services on 2 January 1952.

Periods of hiring since then have usually been as a result of industrial action — even during the war, in April 1944, when a limited strike by crews saw the army stepping in on routes 6 and 581 using lorries with hastily applied chalked route information.

The bus strike that dragged on throughout much of May and June 1958 saw the LTE granting permission for other operators to apply for licences to run services. This took place only on a limited scale, with a few independents running on a handful of routes: Chiltern Queens, for instance, ran a service between Chiswick and Hyde Park Corner. More prominent were the buses hired to the right-wing People's League for the Defence of

Above:
One of the vehicles used by the People's League for the Defence of Freedom during the 1958 bus strike was FT 5702, a Weymann-bodied AEC Regent new to Tynemouth & District in 1946, similar in appearance to the last batch of STLs. Free rides are being offered 'at your own risk', which would date this picture to between 31 May and 13 June, after which a flat fare of 6d was charged. *V. C. Jones/IAL*

Opposite right:
Over the years, many vehicles have been hired for sightseeing duties, following the withdrawal of LT's own coach fleet in 1963. In red and white livery at Victoria is National Travel London Bedford/Duple BGY 611T. *Kevin Lane*

Opposite below:
Obsolete Fleet OM1, former Midland Red BMMO D9 4903, on Round London Sightseeing duties passing Baker Street station in June 1975, the first season in which these vehicles were operated. *Kevin Lane*

Freedom, which ran seven routes, initially free of charge, but later at a fare of 6d. Vehicles were hired from a dealer and included an ex-Leicester AEC Renown and a number of elderly Leylands originating from Lytham St Annes and East Kent.

Another occasion where independent operators have provided cover for services disrupted by industrial action was in January and February 1966. An overtime and rest day working ban was imposed with the result that many routes were either withdrawn or curtailed, with other operators allowed to run these sections. Although permission was not given for other routes to be supplemented, this did take place, but fares could not be charged. Over 20 coach operators ran these services, often using vehicles laid up over the winter. The passenger who usually travelled to work in an RT might find a modern Bedford VAL in its place; not such a hardship! Most of the routes returned to LT operation, although one or two routes did pass to the temporary operator: Isleworth Coaches, for instance, retained the 235 up Richmond Hill, using moreover an RTL.

From June 1972 London Transport hired several open-top Guy Arabs from East Kent to work on the Round London sightseeing tour. Operated under contract by Samuelsons, they were driven by East Kent drivers, with LT conductors. Maintained by Samuelsons they were garaged at LT's Camberwell garage.

From April 1975, London Transport began hiring open-top vehicles in the form of ex-Midland Red D9s from Obsolete Fleet, London W1, for use on the Round London Sightseeing Tours (RLST). These were numbered OM1-7, with closed top, OM8-10 being added in 1980. Obsolete Fleet also supplied buses for other tours, including 'Back Street London', using a former Northern General Routemaster and 'Vintage Bus Route 100', the latter usually employing former London Transport ST922. Other double-deckers hired to work the RLST included four London Country AN class Leyland Atlanteans painted into LT red livery, while other types, including the ubiquitous DMS, have been operated on hire. There has since been a dramatic increase in the number of operators running sightseeing trips, many still using DMSs.

Over the years, London has played host to a number of demonstrating vehicles. Some of these have been mentioned under the class to which they apply, in many cases, particularly in later years, their appearance being followed by a batch of similar vehicles for service. On other occasions a subsequent order might not have been forthcoming, such vehicles moving on to another operator to become a 'might have been' where London is concerned.

The 1950s saw several single-deckers hired to London Transport for demonstration purposes. After the war a new generation of saloon for bus and Green Line service was sought. AEC provided its prototype AEC Regal IV, registered UMP 227 and fitted with a Park Royal 40-seat body. It went into service at St Albans as a 36-seater in May 1950, staying until September 1951 when it returned to AEC, where it was used for works transport, passing into preservation some 20 years later. This bus, of course, preceded the 715-strong RF/RFW classes.

By the time that the RFs had settled in, lightweight underfloor-engined chassis were becoming popular. There was still a small single-deck requirement on top of that filled by the RFs and, rather than order a few more of these now outdated buses, comparative trials took place during 1953-4 between three lightweights: the Bristol LS, Leyland PSUC1/1 Tiger Cub and the AEC Monocoach.

447
GREEN LINE
RG130
NLP 635

99
TEA
FROM THE CO-OP
4
CANTERBURY
Face the future with PEARL assurance
254 CLT

complete with a bullseye on the front dash, certainly looked the part. Like all of the lightweights, it worked from Reigate on routes 447 and 711 and included a stint on Central Area routes 208/208A.

Leyland Tiger Cub PSUC1/1 carried a Saunders-Roe 44-seat body and was registered PTE 592, arriving on loan in June 1953. It was a proper demonstrator and was also finished in Green Line livery. Finally came the AEC Monocoach, an integral design with a 44-seat Park Royal body, and also a proper demonstrator. It arrived in the July and was registered NLP 634. Although this bus moved on with the other two in April 1954, it returned to London Transport in 1956-7 on route 447 having had its pre-selective gearbox replaced by a new Monocontrol semi-automatic transmission.

While there may well have been a clear winner in these trials, by the time that any conclusion may have been reached, the vehicle requirement had decreased and thus further vehicles were not needed. Three lightweight saloons did enter the fleet at a later date, however: the RW class of AEC Reliances of 1960.

Although Routemaster production was in full swing, London Transport received another AEC type as a demonstrator in 1962. Park Royal-bodied AEC Renown 8071 ML was trialled in the Country Area from Northfleet garage for a period, actually receiving the number RX1. Its lack of interest with London Transport was reflected elsewhere, with only 252 being built until 1967. RX1 subsequently passed to the Essex independent, Osbourne of Tollesbury, and was later preserved.

It should perhaps be mentioned that London Transport buses have served as demonstrators themselves. RT19 served as a demonstrator for AEC during 1940-42, while the prototype forward-entrance Routemaster, RMF1254, ran for Liverpool and Manchester Corporations and East Kent in 1962-3 before being trialled with BEA and eventually sold to Northern General. Manchester also received RM1414 on loan in 1963. In later years, vehicles would be loaned to an operator for evaluation when large numbers of buses were rendered surplus; for example, Strathclyde PTE took BL22 in 1981, but no sales resulted. A more recent example was the use of Titans T47/148/217 during 1992 as a run up to the initial sale of the class. One of the operators who sampled the delights of the Titan was Stuart Palmer Travel, Dunstable, which had T217 in the December. Stuart Palmer apparently found it too complicated and ended up buying more DMSs instead!

An interesting vehicle was demonstrated by Hestair-Dennis in 1977. This was a former Leeds Corporation Daimler CVG6 with Roe bodywork, registered 7517 UA and new in 1959. It was used between the July and September on route 27 from Turnham Green garage as a testbed for the combination of Gardner 6LXB engine

PHW 918, a 45-seat ECW-bodied Bristol LS5G, arrived in March 1953, having been new to Bristol Tramways & Carriage Co a month earlier. It was not strictly a demonstrator as it was Tilling policy to put out its vehicles to other members of the group, London Transport now was, like Tilling, part of the British Transport Commission. The bus, finished in Green Line livery and

Opposite top:
Representing the trials of lightweight saloons which took place during 1953-54 is AEC Monocoach/Park Royal NLP 635, working from Reigate garage on route 447 (Redhill-Woldingham). *Kevin Lane Collection*

Opposite below:
The prototype forward-entrance Routemaster RMF1254 was demonstrated to East Kent Road Car in March 1963, seen here at Canterbury. *Kevin Lane Collection*

Above:
Titan T217 was used as a demonstrator to potential buyers of the type in 1992. In the December it ran with Stuart Palmer Travel, Dunstable, where it is seen working route S38 between Lewsey Farm and Downside Estate. Stuart Palmer was not impressed enough to take any, T217 ending up with Merseybus. *Kevin Lane*

and Voith Diwa automatic transmission. This driveline became standard in the Dennis Dominator, then in development, though more significantly for LT — and ironically for Dennis — it also became standard in the MCW Metrobus.

There have been other interesting buses demonstrated in London, particularly in recent years. London Buses has tried many of the more modern types, mini and midibuses in particular, a few of which have been taken into stock. Some have been used in service, and occasionally given fleet numbers, while others have visited garages for inspection only. Their period of demonstration was usually brief and so they have been sometimes quite elusive to the enthusiast. A few of the more interesting loans are detailed below.

The year 1986 saw a Northern Counties-bodied Dennis Domino hired from Greater Manchester Transport. No 1760 (C760 YBA) was numbered DMB1 on paper and was used on route C11 as a possible replacement for the BLs. As it turned out, the BLs soldiered on until R&I Tours took over the route in 1990 using the ubiquitous Dennis Dart.

Dennis Darts have been demonstrated in their various forms. In 1990, for instance, G895 XPX, with Wadham Stringer 'Portsdown' bodywork was used in service as was the Wright Handybus-bodied Dart JDZ 2300 which managed to arrive after the actual production vehicles, DW1-14. It later became DW100, though at first it was oddly numbered DW00 by Wright's. Larger single-deck vehicles in recent years have included the Leyland Lynx, DAF-Optare Delta, MAN-Optare Vecta and a Scania/Plaxton Verde.

In April and May 1992, South Yorkshire Transport loaned one of its Leyland DAB articulated 'Bendibuses', C101 HDT, to Selkent where it operated on route 180 from Plumstead garage. This was the first time that such a vehicle had been used in normal service in London.

Double-deck demonstrators have not featured so much, although one interesting exception was Leyland Olympian J248 WWK, a massive six-wheel Alexander-bodied 'Megadecker', which was on its way to be delivered to Citybus of Hong Kong in 1992. It ran on route 180 for a couple of weeks during July and August, receiving a special dispensation to do so.

Training buses have traditionally been drawn from the ranks of obsolete classes when their passenger days are done. There have, however, been some deviations from this practice. In 1978 there was a severe shortage of trainers due to unserviceable RTs and the late arrival from London Country of Routemasters destined for

Below:
Greater Manchester Dennis Domino 1760 in use by London Buses early in 1986 on BL route C11. It is seen heading for Brent Cross in Belsize Park. *Kevin Lane*

Opposite top:
Many minibuses have been hired in recent years. Six Ivecos, E291-6 VOM, were on loan in 1988 when E296 VOM is seen on route 153 heading towards Archway station that November. It carries both London Buses and Carlyle Group legal lettering. This bus later became Southend Transport 412. *Kevin Lane*

Opposite middle:
One of the more outstanding 'demonstrators' to operate in London was C101 HDT, a South Yorkshire Transport Leyland-DAB articulated 'Bendibus'. It was trialled by Selkent from April 1992 on route 180 from Plumstead garage and was photographed in Romney Road, Greenwich. *Graham Wise*

Opposite bottom
LE1, the Leyland Titan PD2/40 new to Warrington Corporation in 1964, standing outside London Coaches' Wandsworth garage in January 1990. *Kevin Lane Collection*

this role. This led to the hiring of a number of preserved RTs and RTLs, 17 in total, at various times between April and November. On other odd occasions vehicles have been hired for specific training purposes, such as the use of Bristol FLF/ECW EHT 108C at Harrow Weald in June 1991 to acquaint drivers with the manual gearbox. With the profusion of mini and midibus classes from the late 1980s, a number of smaller minibuses were also hired for training purposes during this period.

Acquired, rather than hired, training buses outside the main classes have brought from private owners a couple of notable vehicles into the fleet. In 1986, London Coaches bought AED 26B, a former Warrington Corporation manual-gearbox Leyland PD2/40 with East Lancs bodywork. It was given the number LE1. Another manual-gearbox double-decker to be acquired by London Buses was RV1, a former East Kent AEC Regent V/Park Royal. Registered GJG 750D, it went to Leaside Buses at Stamford Hill for school, private hire and driver training duties. A number of coaches have also been bought for training purposes.

Mention of coaches reminds us of the Bedford VAL with Plaxton bodywork owned by London Transport from 1975 until 1981. New in 1967 and registered RUW 990E to Homerton Coaches, E9, it was used for twin-steer experiments at Chiswick. It was sold and converted into a caravan for a Northamptonshire owner and re-registered KBD 453Y. Another member of the service fleet recruited outside London Transport was Leyland National mobile shop 1234L, new to Plymouth City Transport and acquired by LT in 1982 to replace former SMS753, converted in 1978.

Above:
Leaside's AEC Regent RV1 heads along the A5 through Dunstable bound for a day out at Showbus in 1992, followed by a selection of other London types including DRL41. *Kevin Lane*

Below:
In 1983 a former Plymouth City Transport Leyland National, SCO 422L, was acquired as a replacement for SPB753 (ex-SMS753), the sales and information bus. Numbered 1234L, it was seen inside Victoria garage in December 1983. *Kevin Lane*

London Buses: Privatisation and After

The former London Buses Ltd operations were largely sold to the private sector during 1994 (the sale of South London was not completed until January 1995, while London Coaches was privatised back in May 1992). Prior to their sale, there was a certain autonomy to the various units, allowing them their own say in vehicle purchasing policy. After privatisation, the new companies were able fully to go their own way, although those sold into established groups, such as Stagecoach, would see the stamp of company policy in new acquisitions. Livery styles on buses working in central London had to be 80 per cent based on the old red, although each company is settling down to its chosen image: Metroline have chosen to include a blue skirt, for instance. These words are written some 18 months into the new order, and it might be interesting to see how events, as far as the vehicles are concerned, have taken over the new companies.

London Coaches, sold to its management in May 1992, was composed at the time of mostly Routemasters for sightseeing duties, and an assortment of Van Hool-bodied DAF coaches, occupied with private hire and commuter work. Other coaches included further DAFs, Volvos and a couple of Leyland Tigers, while there were the Ikarus-bodied DAFs used on the 726, the Leyland PD2 trainer and three Dennis Dominators, H1-3. Four years on, there is still a sizeable Routemaster allocation, supported by open-top Metroliners, open and closed-top Willowbrook-bodied Bristol VRs (ex-East Kent) and several ex-London Metrobuses. Van Hool-bodied DAFs still feature, while the Ikarus-bodied DAFs have been increased from 10 to 13. Several of these together with the other DAFs are used on North Kent Express commuter services, operated as a separate company, London Coaches (Kent) Ltd. This is not the whole story of course; interesting developments during this period have included the operation of tendered route 52 with Leyland Titans.

The first bus operator to be sold was Westlink, bought by its management in January 1994 only to be sold to West Midlands Travel in April of the same year. It was sold to London United Busways in September 1995. At its original sale, the fleet was largely single-deck, composed of LS, DA, DWL, CV, MR, MRL and FS types, together with the T class Leyland Titans used on the 131. The CVs have subsequently been withdrawn, while the Titans were replaced by London United's VA class Alexander-bodied Volvo Olympians during 1996. Other new buses have been MAN-Optare Vectas, new in 1995.

The majority of the former London Buses fleets were sold off during the autumn of 1994. CentreWest was sold to its management on 2 September. The inherited fleet consisted of RMLs, together with a handful of RMs and two RMCs, and a quantity of Ms making up the double-deckers. There was more variety in the single-deckers: DW, LLW, LS, GLS, LX, MA, RW, MT, MTL and MW classes all being represented. There were also no fewer than 15 BL driver trainers in stock. Subsequent additions are Volvo Olympians, Dennis Darts and Marshall-bodied Mercedes. CentreWest now operates tendered routes well out of its area, in Orpington, while Beeline and London Buslines were acquired along with around 200 vehicles in March 1996, perhaps indicating the way forward for some of these new companies.

Selkent was bought by Stagecoach on 6 September. The majority of vehicles were Titans, followed by Olympians, with two RMCs and two DMs the only other double-deckers. There was a proliferation of saloon and midibus classes: LA, LV, DT, DW, MR, MRL, RH, FM, MA, MC, MT, MTL and MW. There were also eight DAF coaches. Changes under the new regime have included the delivery of 52 new Volvo Olympians, thus allowing the withdrawal of some Titans. The LAs have been transferred to Stagecoach East London and thence out of London, to Ribble, and the FM and MW classes have also gone following the loss of their 'Roundabout' network at Orpington in December 1995. A number of new Dennis Darts have also entered the fleet. The DAF coaches and the DMs have all gone, with the only Routemaster being open-top RMC1515.

On the same date, Stagecoach also took East London, in a combined deal with Selkent. Here, Routemasters were much in evidence — mostly RMLs, but including a sprinkling of RM, RMA and RMC variants. There were plenty of Titans too, this part of London being their traditional stamping ground. Other double-deck classes were Scanias and a lone Optare Spectra, SP2. As with Selkent, there were a number of single-deck classes, in this case DA, SLW, DRL, DW, DWL, MR, MRL and SR. Three coaches were a pair of Leyland Tigers and a Volvo B10M. New for Stagecoach East London have been Dennis Darts, including SLFs and a large number of Volvo Olympians. Also, as noted above, LAs have been transferred from Selkent. Notable is RMC1461, restored to traditional Green Line livery but still available for service.

Leaside Buses became part of the Cowie Group on 29 September 1994. The initial fleet was mostly double-deck, with Metrobuses well in the majority. Routemasters were almost all RMLs, with two RMCs and the lone RM5. Forty Olympians were also on the books, with three DMSs, including one open-topper, five Titans and RV1, the AEC Regent driver trainer. Single-deckers were SLW, DRL, MR and SR classes, with a pair of Leyland Leopard coaches completing the fleet. New buses have been DAF/Northern Counties double-deckers and the ubiquitous Dennis Dart. Further coaches are now in stock and an acquisition is a former London Country Atlantean, now an open-topper.

Metroline was the subject of a management buyout on 7 October 1994. Metrobuses and RMLs were in the majority, although there were a large number of DR and DT Dennis Darts. Of lesser numbers were LN, SR, LLW and MR classes. There was also a single coach, Leyland Leopard LD5. Further Darts have been bought, with more currently on order. November 1994 saw the acquisition of Atlas Bus, its Titans being retained for route 52 although these have been replaced by Volvo Olympians, while the Brents Travel Group, Watford, together with over 30 coaches, was taken over in October 1995.

London Northern was sold to MTL Holdings on 26 October 1994, soon to become MTL London. At privatisation the fleet consisted of RM, RML, S, V, DNL, DRL, MRL, MW and SR types, together with two DMSs (one open-top and one trainer), four delicensed LSs, a Volvo coach and a Neoplan Skyliner. Olympians and ex-London Titans were added to the fleet with the takeover of GEMSAM Holdings, which included London Suburban Buses, in April 1995. Furthermore, R&I Tours of Acton was acquired in October 1995, bringing with it a large fleet including Dennis Darts and MAN/Optare Vectas. New vehicles include Marshall-bodied MANs.

The management and employee buyout of London General went through on 2 November 1994. Large numbers of Metrobuses were joined by RMLs, while other classes consisted of VC, VN, LS, GLS, DR, DRL, DW, MA, MRL and MT. In addition, there were DMS trainers and SC1, also a training bus. The only new buses by the spring of 1996 were 16 Dennis Darts.

London United was sold to its management on 5 November 1994. Its opening fleet consisted of Routemast ers, mainly RMLs, plus M, L, LLW, LX, DR, DRL, DT, FR and MRL classes. New

buses have been bought for Airbus duties in the shape of Volvo Olympians with Alexander Royale air-conditioned bodywork. As noted above, Westlink was acquired in September 1995.

The sale of London Central to the Go-Ahead Group was completed on 18 November 1994, with RM, RML, T, L, SP, DRL, DEL, MR, MRL, SR and MTL classes represented. Volvo Olympians with Alexander and Northern Counties bodywork have been added to stock during 1995-6, these representing the first new double-deckers to be purchased by a former LBL company.

The privatisation of London Buses was completed with the sale of South London to the Cowie Group, already the owner of Leaside. Very much a double-deck dominated fleet, large numbers of Routemasters and Metrobuses were operated along with Olympians and a handful of Titans. Midibuses were of MR, MRL, SR, DR, DRL and DT classes. Further Darts were added in 1996.

Below:
The enthusiast, perhaps visiting London for the first time since the privatisation of London Buses, will see many changes. True, the vehicles of the former London Buses companies are still largely red; but for how long? The familiar roundel has gone, replaced by the identity of the new operator. Although the former vehicle classification has been continued, numbering of new types has not always been by this system. A case in point is MTL London 209 at Liverpool Street in November 1996. MTL, which bought London Northern in October 1994, also acquired London Suburban Bus in April 1995. Among its fleet was a batch of Northern Counties-bodied Volvo Olympians, numbered 201-19. Here 209 is working LRT tendered route 271 to Highgate Village, at a relatively new bus station down the side of the rebuilt Liverpool Street station. The buildings behind are built on the site of the old Broad Street station. *Kevin Lane*

Bibliography

Adlam, James and Hamer, Keith: *DMS Handbook*; Capital Transport Publishing, 1994.

Arnold, Barry and Harris, Mike: *Reshaping London's Buses*; Capital Transport Publishing, 1982.

Blacker, Ken: *RT*; Capital Transport Publishing, 1979.

Blacker, Ken: *Routemaster, Volumes 1/2*; Capital Transport Publishing, 1991-92.

Blake, Jim: *RT Twilight*; Regent Transport Publishing, 1978.

Blake, Jim and Turner, Barry: *At London's Service*; The Regent Press, 1983.

Blake, Jim and Williamson, R. J.: *Routemaster Roundabout*; Regent Transport Publishing, 1981.

Carman, W. J.: *Channel Islands Transport, Vol 2*; W. J. Carman, 1995.

Curtis, Colin: *Buses Of London*; London Transport, 1979.

Gascoine, Peter: *The London RLH Remembered*; Roadmaster Publishing, 1995.

Glazier, Ken: *London Buses Before The War*; Capital Transport Publishing, 1995.

Glazier, Ken: *London Buses In The 1950s*; Capital Transport Publishing, 1989.

Hambley, John: *London Transport Buses & Coaches*; John Hambley, various editions.

Joyce, J.: *London Transport Bus Garages Since 1948*; Ian Allan Ltd, 1988.

Lane, Kevin: *Bus & Coach Recognition: London's Buses*; Ian Allan Ltd, 1991.

Millar, Alan: *Bus & Coach Recognition*; Ian Allan Ltd, 1992.

Mills, G. R. and Burnett, J.: *Londoners In Exile*; Roadliner Transport Books, 1984.

Mills, G. R. and Nicholson, R. W.: *London Buses In Exile*; Bus Enthusiast Publishing, 1991.

Morgan, Andrew: *Routemaster Handbook*; Capital Transport Publishing, 1992 and 1996.

Reed, John: *London Buses Past And Present*; Capital Transport Publishing, 1994.

Reed, John: *RT Jubilee*; Silver Link Publishing, 1989.

Robbins, George and Thomas, Alan: *London Buses Between The Wars*; Marshall Harris and Baldwin, 1980.

Stenning, Ray and Whelan, Trevor: *A London Country Bus Album*; Viewfinder, 1977.

Stenning, Ray and Whelan, Trevor: *A London RF Album*; Viewfinder, 1977.

Stewart, David: *London Country*; Capital Transport Publishing, 1984.

Wise, Graham: *Bus & Coach Recognition: Veteran & Vintage*; Ian Allan Ltd, 1989.

Various editions of the following publications were also used:

British Bus Fleets, London Transport; Ian Allan Ltd

Buses/Buses Extra; Ian Allan Ltd

Buses Annual/Buses Yearbook, Ian Allan Ltd

Buses Of London Fleetbooks; LOTS

London Transport Buses; Capital Transport Publishing

London Bus Magazine; LOTS

London Bus Review; LOTS

London Transport Fleet Histories; PSV Circle